Sustainable Happiness: Bhutan's Development and Pursuit of Gross National Happiness

Copyright Page

TITLE: Sustainable Happiness: Bhutan's Development and Pursuit of the Gross National Happiness

1ST Edition

Sustainable Happiness: Bhutan's Development and the Pursuit of Gross National Happiness

By Roberto Miguel Rodriguez

Chapter 1: Introduction to Bhutan and Gross National Happiness

Bhutan's unique approach to development and happiness

Bhutan's unique approach to development and happiness has captivated the world's attention. Nestled in the heart of the Himalayas, this small kingdom has made remarkable strides in achieving sustainable happiness through its Gross National Happiness (GNH) philosophy. For travelers seeking a deeper understanding of Bhutanese culture, spirituality, and sustainable development, exploring these facets becomes a transformative journey.

Bhutanese spirituality and meditation practices form the bedrock of the country's approach to happiness. Travelers can immerse themselves in the ancient traditions of Buddhism, learning meditation techniques from revered monks and discovering inner peace in breathtaking monasteries and meditation retreats. These practices offer a glimpse into the profound spiritual connection that underpins Bhutanese society.

Bhutanese traditional arts and crafts are another treasure trove waiting to be explored. From intricate woodcarvings to vibrant thangka paintings, travelers can witness the expertise of Bhutanese artisans firsthand. Engaging in workshops and visiting local artisans' studios allows visitors to gain a deeper appreciation for the craftsmanship and preserve these centuries-old traditions.

Bhutanese cuisine and culinary traditions offer a mouthwatering adventure for food enthusiasts. Delight in the flavors of ema datshi, a spicy chili and cheese dish, or momos, delectable dumplings filled with meat or vegetables. Travelers can also learn the art of Bhutanese cooking through immersive culinary experiences, using locally sourced ingredients and traditional cooking techniques.

Bhutanese festivals and cultural celebrations provide a window into the vibrant tapestry of Bhutanese culture. Colorful dances, masked performances, and sacred rituals mark these occasions. Joining in the festivities during the Tshechu festivals or witnessing the grandeur of the Punakha Drubchen allows travelers to witness the living traditions that bring the Bhutanese people together.

For adventure seekers, Bhutanese trekking and adventure tourism offer unparalleled experiences. Traverse the pristine landscapes of the Himalayas, trekking through dense forests, high mountain passes, and picturesque valleys. Encounter rare wildlife, including the elusive snow leopard and the majestic takin, Bhutan's national animal.

Bhutan's commitment to biodiversity and wildlife conservation is laudable. Travelers can visit national parks and conservation areas to witness the country's efforts firsthand. Learn about Bhutan's conservation success stories, such as the protection of the rare black-necked crane, and contribute to the preservation of its rich biodiversity.

Bhutanese traditional medicine and alternative healing practices are deeply rooted in the country's culture. Travelers can explore the ancient healing techniques of traditional medicine, including herbal remedies, hot stone baths, and acupuncture. Discover the holistic approach to wellness that complements Bhutan's pursuit of happiness.

Bhutanese architecture and traditional building techniques showcase the country's commitment to sustainable development. Explore the intricately designed dzongs, fortress-like structures that serve as administrative and religious centers. Witness the harmony between nature and architecture in Bhutan's unique vernacular buildings, constructed using traditional methods and eco-friendly materials.

Bhutanese textile and weaving traditions are a testament to the country's rich cultural heritage. Travelers can visit weaving centers and witness the meticulous process of creating intricate patterns and motifs. Purchase exquisite textiles, including the famous kushuthara, and support the preservation of this ancient craft.

Finally, Bhutanese sustainable development and GNH philosophy provide invaluable lessons for travelers. Engage in discussions with local experts and policymakers to understand how Bhutan has prioritized happiness and well-being over material wealth. Learn about Bhutan's initiatives in renewable energy, organic farming, and community-based tourism, and discover how these practices contribute to a sustainable and harmonious society.

Embarking on a journey through Bhutan's development and happiness is an enlightening experience for travelers. By immersing oneself in Bhutanese spirituality, arts, cuisine, festivals, trekking, biodiversity, medicine, architecture, textiles, and sustainable development, one gains a profound appreciation for the country's unique approach to happiness and its commitment to preserving its cultural and natural heritage.

Overview of the Gross National Happiness philosophy

The Gross National Happiness (GNH) philosophy is a unique approach to development that originated in the small Himalayan kingdom of Bhutan. Unlike conventional measures of progress that focus solely on economic growth, Bhutan's GNH philosophy emphasizes holistic well-being and sustainable happiness. This subchapter provides an overview of the GNH philosophy for travelers interested in understanding the unique values and principles that shape Bhutanese society.

At its core, the GNH philosophy aims to strike a balance between material and spiritual development. Bhutan recognizes that economic growth alone does not guarantee happiness and well-being. Instead, the country places equal importance on non-economic factors such as cultural preservation, environmental conservation, and good governance.

One key aspect of the GNH philosophy is Bhutanese spirituality and meditation practices. Visitors can delve into the country's spiritual traditions, which are deeply rooted in Buddhism. Bhutan offers numerous meditation retreats and spiritual centers where travelers can engage in mindfulness practices and gain insights into the Bhutanese way of life.

Bhutanese traditional arts and crafts are also integral to the GNH philosophy. The country is renowned for its intricate thangka paintings, wood carvings, and hand-woven textiles. Travelers can explore the rich artistic heritage of Bhutan through visits to local artisans and craft workshops.

Bhutanese cuisine and culinary traditions reflect the GNH philosophy as well. The emphasis on organic and locally sourced ingredients promotes sustainable farming practices and supports local communities. Travelers can savor the unique flavors of Bhutanese cuisine, which often incorporates spicy chilies, cheese, and traditional dishes like ema datshi (chili and cheese stew).

Bhutanese festivals and cultural celebrations are another manifestation of the GNH philosophy. These vibrant events showcase the country's rich cultural heritage and provide opportunities for visitors to immerse themselves in Bhutanese traditions. From the colorful Paro Tshechu to the lively Punakha Drubchen, these festivals offer a glimpse into the Bhutanese way of life.

For adventure enthusiasts, Bhutanese trekking and adventure tourism offer opportunities to witness the country's breathtaking landscapes. The

GNH philosophy ensures that tourism activities are sustainable and promote environmental conservation.

Bhutan's commitment to biodiversity and wildlife conservation is another aspect of the GNH philosophy. Travelers can explore the country's diverse ecosystems, including protected areas like the Royal Manas National Park, and learn about Bhutan's efforts to preserve its unique flora and fauna.

The GNH philosophy also encompasses Bhutanese traditional medicine and alternative healing practices. Visitors can discover the healing power of herbal remedies and holistic therapies, which have been used in Bhutan for centuries.

Bhutanese architecture and traditional building techniques are another intriguing aspect of the GNH philosophy. Travelers can admire the country's distinctive dzongs (fortresses), monasteries, and traditional houses, which showcase the harmonious blend of aesthetics and functionality.

Lastly, Bhutanese textile and weaving traditions reflect the GNH philosophy's focus on preserving cultural heritage. Visitors can witness the intricate process of creating hand-woven textiles, adorned with vibrant patterns and colors.

In conclusion, the GNH philosophy shapes various aspects of Bhutanese society, from spirituality and traditional arts to cuisine and sustainable development. By embracing the GNH philosophy, travelers can gain a deeper understanding of Bhutan's unique approach to happiness and well-being, making their journey not only an adventure but also a transformative experience.

Bhutan's commitment to sustainable development

Bhutan, famously known as "The Mysterious Kingdom," has long been an enigma to travelers from around the world. Nestled in the heart of the mighty Himalayas, this small landlocked country has captured the imagination of adventurers and spiritual seekers alike. But what truly sets Bhutan apart is its unwavering commitment to sustainable development.

In the pursuit of Gross National Happiness (GNH), Bhutan's unique development philosophy, the country has placed environmental conservation and sustainable practices at the core of its policies. This commitment stems from the belief that true happiness can only be achieved by harmonizing economic growth with social and environmental well-being.

One of the most remarkable aspects of Bhutan's sustainable development efforts is its dedication to preserving its pristine natural environment. With over 70% of its land covered by forests, Bhutan is often referred to as the "Green Jewel of the Himalayas." The country has implemented stringent policies to ensure the preservation of its biodiversity, including a constitutional mandate to maintain at least 60% forest coverage at all times. This commitment has led to the creation of numerous national parks and conservation areas, protecting endangered species such as the elusive snow leopard and the majestic Royal Bengal tiger.

Bhutan's commitment to sustainability goes beyond just environmental conservation. The country has made significant strides in promoting renewable energy sources, aiming to achieve carbon neutrality by 2030. Hydropower, with its abundant supply of fast-flowing rivers, is Bhutan's primary source of energy, meeting the country's domestic needs while exporting excess electricity to neighboring countries. This emphasis on renewable energy not only reduces Bhutan's reliance on fossil fuels but also contributes to the global fight against climate change.

Furthermore, Bhutan's commitment to sustainable development is reflected in its approach to tourism. The government strictly regulates the number of tourists allowed into the country each year, ensuring that the industry does not harm the environment or the unique culture of Bhutan. Travelers to Bhutan are required to book their trips through authorized tour operators, who are committed to providing sustainable and responsible tourism experiences. This approach allows visitors to immerse themselves in the beauty of Bhutan while minimizing their impact on the environment and supporting local communities.

In conclusion, Bhutan's commitment to sustainable development sets it apart as a truly unique destination. As travelers, we have the privilege of experiencing the breathtaking landscapes, rich cultural heritage, and warm hospitality of this mysterious kingdom. By embracing Bhutan's sustainable practices and supporting its pursuit of Gross National Happiness, we can contribute to the preservation of this remarkable country for future generations to enjoy.

Chapter 2: Bhutanese Spirituality and Meditation Practices

Understanding the importance of spirituality in Bhutanese culture

Bhutan, often referred to as the "Land of the Thunder Dragon," is a country renowned for its unique cultural heritage and commitment to preserving its traditions. At the heart of Bhutanese culture lies spirituality, which plays a significant role in shaping the lives of its people and the nation as a whole. Understanding the importance of spirituality in Bhutanese culture is essential for travelers seeking a deeper connection with this enchanting land.

Spirituality in Bhutan is deeply rooted in Buddhism, the country's predominant religion. Bhutanese spirituality encompasses a holistic approach to life, emphasizing the cultivation of inner peace, harmony, and wisdom. Visitors to Bhutan have the opportunity to witness and partake in various spiritual practices, including meditation, prayer, and rituals performed in monasteries and temples scattered across the country.

Bhutanese spirituality and meditation practices offer travelers a chance to embark on a journey of self-discovery and inner transformation. By immersing themselves in the serene ambiance of a monastery or participating in meditation retreats, visitors can experience a sense of tranquility and gain insights into their own spiritual paths.

Beyond its religious significance, spirituality in Bhutan also intertwines with various aspects of everyday life, including traditional arts and crafts, cuisine, festivals, and architecture. Bhutanese traditional arts and crafts, such as thangka painting, wood carving, and statue making, are not mere artistic expressions but spiritual practices that foster mindfulness and devotion.

Similarly, Bhutanese cuisine and culinary traditions are deeply influenced by spiritual beliefs. The use of organic, locally sourced ingredients and the practice of mindful eating reflect the Bhutanese reverence for nature and the interconnectedness of all living beings.

Bhutanese festivals and cultural celebrations provide a glimpse into the rich spiritual heritage of the country. These vibrant events, such as the annual Tsechu festivals, feature colorful dances, music, and rituals that celebrate the teachings of Buddhism and honor the country's spiritual guardians.

For adventure-seeking travelers, Bhutan offers unparalleled trekking opportunities amidst its breathtaking landscapes. Trekking in Bhutan is not just a physical endeavor but a spiritual journey that allows visitors to connect with nature, contemplate their place in the world, and experience a sense of awe and reverence for the natural world.

Bhutan's commitment to preserving its natural environment and biodiversity is also deeply rooted in spirituality. The country's emphasis on sustainable development and wildlife conservation reflects its belief in the intrinsic value of all forms of life and the interconnectedness of human well-being and the environment.

Furthermore, Bhutanese traditional medicine and alternative healing practices, known as Sowa Rigpa, are deeply intertwined with spirituality. These ancient healing techniques, which utilize herbal remedies and energy balancing, promote holistic well-being and seek to restore harmony between body, mind, and spirit.

Bhutanese architecture and traditional building techniques also embody spiritual principles. The design of monasteries, dzongs (fortresses), and traditional houses reflects the belief in sacred geometry and the harmonious integration of human-made structures with the natural environment.

Lastly, Bhutanese textile and weaving traditions carry spiritual significance, with intricate patterns and motifs representing auspicious symbols and spiritual teachings. The art of weaving serves as a meditative practice, generating positive energy and promoting mindfulness.

Understanding the importance of spirituality in Bhutanese culture is essential for travelers seeking to immerse themselves in the country's rich heritage. By embracing Bhutan's spiritual traditions, visitors can embark on a transformative journey, connecting with the inner self, nature, and the profound wisdom that has shaped this remarkable nation.

Exploring the practices of meditation and mindfulness

In the pursuit of sustainable happiness, the tiny kingdom of Bhutan offers a wealth of ancient wisdom and practices that can transform our lives. Among these practices are meditation and mindfulness, which have been deeply rooted in Bhutanese spirituality for centuries. For travelers seeking a meaningful and transformative experience, exploring the practices of meditation and mindfulness in Bhutan can provide a profound connection to the country's rich cultural heritage.

Meditation is a practice that involves training the mind to focus and redirect thoughts. It is often accompanied by mindfulness, which involves being fully present and aware of one's thoughts, feelings, and surroundings. In Bhutan, meditation and mindfulness are deeply ingrained in everyday life, and the Bhutanese people view them as essential tools for cultivating inner peace and happiness.

Travelers interested in Bhutanese spirituality and meditation practices can embark on guided retreats and workshops that offer a unique opportunity to learn from experienced meditation masters. These retreats often take place in serene monasteries and meditation centers nestled in the breathtaking landscapes of Bhutan. Participants can immerse themselves in the teachings of ancient Buddhist texts, learn various meditation techniques, and experience the transformative power of silence and solitude.

Furthermore, these retreats provide a space for travelers to connect with like-minded individuals from around the world, fostering a sense of community and shared growth. The meditative practices learned during these retreats can be carried back into everyday life, serving as tools for stress reduction, emotional well-being, and personal growth.

In addition to meditation and mindfulness, Bhutan offers a range of other practices that promote holistic well-being. These include Bhutanese traditional arts and crafts, which are deeply rooted in spiritual traditions and provide a means for self-expression and creativity. Travelers can engage in workshops to learn traditional painting, sculpture, or wood carving, and gain insight into the symbolic meanings behind these art forms.

Moreover, Bhutanese cuisine and culinary traditions are closely tied to the principles of mindfulness and balance. Travelers can explore the art of mindful eating, savoring every bite as a way to nourish the body and cultivate gratitude. Bhutanese cuisine, with its emphasis on fresh, locally sourced ingredients, offers a unique gastronomic experience that reflects the country's commitment to sustainable living.

The practices of meditation and mindfulness are also deeply integrated into Bhutanese festivals and cultural celebrations. These vibrant events provide an opportunity for travelers to witness the joy and spiritual devotion of the Bhutanese people. Whether it's the colorful dances of the Tshechu festival or the sacred rituals of the Drupchen, these celebrations offer a glimpse into the Bhutanese way of life and the importance of spiritual practices in their pursuit of happiness.

For adventurous travelers, Bhutan offers a range of trekking and adventure tourism opportunities. From the famous Snowman Trek to the picturesque trails of the Jomolhari Trek, these journeys through Bhutan's pristine landscapes provide an opportunity for introspection and connection with nature. Trekking in Bhutan can be a meditative experience, with each step serving as a reminder of the impermanence of life and the importance of being present in the moment.

Bhutan's commitment to biodiversity and wildlife conservation is another aspect that can be explored through meditation and mindfulness. Travelers can engage in eco-tourism activities that promote the preservation of Bhutan's unique flora and fauna, while also cultivating a deeper connection with the natural world. Guided tours to national parks and wildlife sanctuaries offer a chance to practice mindfulness while observing the incredible diversity of Bhutan's ecosystems.

For those interested in alternative healing practices, Bhutanese traditional medicine offers a holistic approach to well-being. Rooted in ancient Buddhist principles and the use of natural herbs and minerals, Bhutanese traditional medicine aims to restore balance and harmony within the body. Travelers can visit traditional medicine centers and learn about the principles of this ancient healing system, which views the mind and body as interconnected.

Bhutanese architecture and traditional building techniques are yet another aspect of the country's cultural heritage that can be explored through the lens of meditation and mindfulness. Travelers can visit ancient monasteries, dzongs (fortresses), and traditional Bhutanese homes, marveling at the intricate woodwork and symbolic design elements. These architectural wonders serve as a reminder of the importance of mindfulness and intention in every aspect of life.

Bhutanese textile and weaving traditions also offer a window into the country's cultural heritage. Travelers can visit weaving centers and witness the intricate process of creating traditional Bhutanese textiles.

Through mindful observation and engagement, travelers can gain a deeper appreciation for the skill and dedication that goes into preserving these ancient techniques.

Lastly, travelers interested in Bhutanese sustainable development and the philosophy of Gross National Happiness (GNH) can explore the intersection of meditation and mindfulness with the country's holistic approach to development. Bhutan's commitment to GNH, which prioritizes well-being and happiness over material wealth, is deeply rooted in spiritual practices. By immersing themselves in Bhutan's meditation and mindfulness practices, travelers can gain insights into the interconnectedness of personal happiness, community well-being, and environmental sustainability.

In summary, exploring the practices of meditation and mindfulness in Bhutan offers travelers a unique opportunity to connect with the country's rich cultural heritage and pursue sustainable happiness. Whether it's learning meditation techniques from experienced masters, engaging in traditional arts and crafts, or immersing oneself in Bhutan's natural landscapes, these practices provide a transformative experience that can enrich both the individual and the wider community. By embracing Bhutan's spiritual traditions, travelers can embark on a journey of self-discovery, personal growth, and a deeper understanding of the interconnectedness of all things.

Learning from Bhutanese spiritual leaders and gurus

Learning from Bhutanese spiritual leaders and gurus offers a unique opportunity to delve into the rich tapestry of Bhutanese spirituality and meditation practices. This subchapter explores the wisdom and teachings of the revered spiritual leaders and gurus, providing invaluable insights for travelers seeking a deeper understanding of Bhutan's spiritual traditions.

Bhutan has long been known as the "Land of the Thunder Dragon," a place where spirituality is deeply ingrained in everyday life. The country's spiritual leaders, known as lamas, have dedicated their lives to the pursuit of enlightenment and guiding others on the path to inner peace and happiness.

By immersing yourself in the teachings of these spiritual leaders, you can gain a greater appreciation for Bhutanese spirituality and the meditation practices that have been passed down through generations. From the art of mindfulness to the practice of compassion, these teachings can have a profound impact on your own spiritual journey.

One of the most renowned spiritual leaders in Bhutan is His Holiness the Je Khenpo, the head of the Bhutanese religious order. His teachings encompass a wide range of topics, including the nature of mind, the importance of ethics, and the pursuit of enlightenment. By learning from the Je Khenpo and other spiritual leaders, travelers can gain a deeper understanding of Bhutanese philosophy and its relevance to their own lives.

In addition to the spiritual teachings, Bhutanese gurus also play a crucial role in preserving and promoting the country's traditional arts and crafts. These gurus are highly skilled in various artistic disciplines such as painting, sculpture, and woodwork. By learning from them, travelers can not only gain insight into the techniques and traditions of Bhutanese art but also support the preservation of these invaluable cultural practices.

Furthermore, Bhutanese spiritual leaders and gurus are often involved in the organization and celebration of festivals and cultural events. By observing and participating in these vibrant celebrations, travelers can witness the unique blend of spirituality, art, and culture that defines Bhutanese society.

Whether you are interested in Bhutanese spirituality, traditional arts and crafts, or simply seeking a deeper understanding of the country's rich cultural heritage, learning from Bhutanese spiritual leaders and gurus offers a transformative experience. Their wisdom, teachings, and guidance can inspire and enlighten travelers on their own quest for sustainable happiness, aligning with Bhutan's philosophy of Gross National Happiness.

Chapter 3: Bhutanese Traditional Arts and Crafts

Appreciating the rich heritage of Bhutanese arts and crafts

Bhutan, a small landlocked country nestled in the mighty Himalayas, is not only famous for its breathtaking landscapes but also for its rich heritage of arts and crafts. For travelers seeking a deeper understanding of Bhutanese culture, exploring its artistic traditions is an essential part of the journey.

Bhutanese spirituality and meditation practices have influenced the country's arts and crafts for centuries. The intricate designs and vibrant colors found in traditional paintings, known as thangkas, are often inspired by Buddhist symbolism and teachings. Travelers can witness the meticulous process of creating these masterpieces, which involves skilled artisans using natural pigments and precious materials like gold and silver.

Bhutanese traditional arts and crafts extend beyond paintings. Wood carving, metalwork, and sculpture are also highly valued artistic practices in Bhutan. Intricately carved wooden masks and statues depict various deities and spiritual beings, reflecting the country's deep-rooted belief in the supernatural. Travelers can visit workshops and witness the craftsmanship firsthand, gaining a deeper appreciation for the skills and dedication behind these creations.

Bhutanese cuisine and culinary traditions are also deeply connected to the country's arts and crafts. Traditional Bhutanese dishes, such as ema datshi (chili and cheese stew) and momo (dumplings), are prepared with great care and artistic flair. Travelers can indulge in these unique flavors while learning about the cultural significance of food in Bhutanese society.

Bhutanese festivals and cultural celebrations provide a window into the country's vibrant artistic traditions. Colorful masked dances, known as tshechus, are performed during religious festivals, showcasing the fusion of art, music, and dance. These events offer travelers a chance to witness the living heritage of Bhutanese arts and crafts, as well as immerse themselves in the lively atmosphere of celebration.

For adventurous travelers, Bhutan offers a unique opportunity to combine trekking and adventure tourism with an appreciation for arts and crafts. Many trekking routes pass through remote villages where traditional weaving and textile traditions are still practiced. Travelers can interact with local weavers, learn about their techniques, and even purchase handmade textiles as souvenirs.

Bhutan's commitment to sustainable development and Gross National Happiness (GNH) philosophy is also reflected in its arts and crafts. The use of natural and locally sourced materials, as well as traditional building techniques, ensures the preservation of cultural heritage and minimizes the environmental impact. By supporting local artisans and purchasing their handicrafts, travelers contribute to the sustainable development of Bhutan's artistic traditions.

In conclusion, exploring the rich heritage of Bhutanese arts and crafts is an enriching experience for travelers seeking a deeper understanding of the country's culture. From thangka paintings to wood carving, Bhutan offers a diverse range of artistic traditions that reflect its spirituality, culinary traditions, festivals, and sustainable development practices. By immersing themselves in Bhutan's artistic legacy, travelers can truly appreciate the depth and beauty of this unique Himalayan kingdom.

Exploring traditional painting and sculpture techniques

Bhutan's rich cultural heritage is deeply intertwined with traditional painting and sculpture techniques, which have been passed down through generations. These art forms not only serve as a means of creative expression but also reflect the country's spiritual beliefs, cultural traditions, and values. In this subchapter, we will delve into the mesmerizing world of Bhutanese traditional painting and sculpture techniques, providing you with insights into the craftsmanship and symbolism behind these art forms.

Bhutanese traditional painting, known as thangka, is a highly intricate and detailed form of art that dates back centuries. Thangkas are religious paintings that depict deities, mandalas, and spiritual motifs. The artists, often monks or skilled artisans, meticulously paint using natural pigments made from minerals and plants. These paintings are not only visually stunning but also serve as a medium for meditation and spiritual contemplation.

Similarly, Bhutanese sculpture is a revered art form. Sculptors employ various techniques to create sculptures of deities, religious figures, and mythological creatures. The materials used range from wood and stone to bronze and clay. Each sculpture is crafted with utmost precision, reflecting the artist's devotion and skill. These sculptures play a significant role in Bhutanese religious practices, adorning temples and monasteries across the country.

By exploring these traditional painting and sculpture techniques, travelers can gain a deeper understanding of Bhutanese spirituality and meditation practices. The intricate details and symbolism behind each artwork offer insights into the country's rich cultural traditions and religious beliefs.

Furthermore, understanding these techniques can also shed light on Bhutanese sustainable development and Gross National Happiness (GNH) philosophy. These art forms, deeply rooted in tradition and spirituality, emphasize the importance of preserving cultural heritage and maintaining a harmonious relationship with the environment.

Whether you are a lover of art, a spiritual seeker, or a cultural enthusiast, delving into Bhutanese traditional painting and sculpture techniques will undoubtedly enrich your travel experience. Witness the masterpieces firsthand, engage with local artists, and immerse yourself in the vibrant world of Bhutanese art. Through this exploration, you will not only gain a deeper appreciation for the country's cultural richness but also contribute to the preservation of these invaluable art forms for future generations to cherish.

Discovering the art of wood carving and metalwork

In the enchanting kingdom of Bhutan, nestled high in the Himalayas, lies a treasure trove of traditional arts and crafts that have been passed down through generations. Among these ancient practices, wood carving and metalwork stand out as intricate and beautiful expressions of Bhutanese culture.

Wood carving in Bhutan is a revered art form that dates back centuries. Skilled craftsmen, often belonging to the Bumthang region, meticulously carve intricate designs into wood, creating stunning masterpieces. These carvings can be found adorning temples, monasteries, and even village homes, adding a touch of elegance and spirituality to the Bhutanese landscape.

The motifs and patterns used in Bhutanese wood carving are deeply rooted in Buddhist symbolism. Dragons, lotus flowers, and mythical creatures are common themes, representing wisdom, purity, and protection. Each piece tells a story, reflecting the rich spiritual heritage of the Bhutanese people.

Metalwork is another art form that holds a special place in Bhutanese culture. Bhutanese metalworkers, known as zorig chusum, use ancient techniques to create intricate sculptures, jewelry, and household items. They work with a variety of metals, including bronze, silver, and gold, using traditional tools and methods that have been passed down through generations.

The art of metalwork often involves intricate filigree and repoussé techniques, where designs are meticulously engraved or embossed onto the metal surface. The end result is a breathtaking piece of art that showcases the skill and creativity of the Bhutanese artisans.

Visitors to Bhutan have the unique opportunity to witness these crafts firsthand. Artisan workshops and studios are scattered throughout the country, providing travelers with a glimpse into the intricate process of wood carving and metalwork. Some even offer hands-on experiences, allowing visitors to try their hand at these ancient crafts under the guidance of skilled artisans.

By immersing yourself in the art of wood carving and metalwork, you not only gain a deeper appreciation for Bhutanese culture but also contribute to the preservation of these traditional practices. Supporting local artisans helps ensure that these crafts continue to thrive and be passed on to future generations.

So, whether you are a traveler seeking spiritual enlightenment, a lover of traditional arts and crafts, or simply curious about Bhutanese culture, discovering the art of wood carving and metalwork is an experience that will leave you in awe of the skill and creativity of the Bhutanese people.

Chapter 4: Bhutanese Cuisine and Culinary Traditions

Introduction to Bhutanese cuisine and its unique flavors

Bhutan, a small landlocked country nestled in the Eastern Himalayas, is renowned for its vibrant culture, breathtaking landscapes, and, of course, its mouthwatering cuisine. Bhutanese cuisine is a delightful blend of flavors, colors, and textures that reflect the country's unique cultural heritage and diverse natural resources. In this chapter, we will take you on a culinary journey through the delectable world of Bhutanese food, exploring its distinctive flavors and the cultural significance of its ingredients.

At the heart of Bhutanese cuisine is the concept of balance and harmony, which is deeply rooted in the country's spiritual traditions. Bhutanese spirituality and meditation practices emphasize the importance of nurturing both the body and the mind, and this philosophy is reflected in the way food is prepared and consumed. Bhutanese meals are typically served with a variety of dishes, each carefully chosen to provide a balanced combination of flavors and nutrients.

One of the most distinctive aspects of Bhutanese cuisine is the use of chili peppers. Bhutanese people love their chilies and believe that it brings good luck and wards off evil spirits. Chili is used not just as a spice, but as a vegetable in its own right, often eaten raw or cooked with meat and vegetables. The unique and fiery taste of Bhutanese chili peppers adds a special kick to their dishes, setting them apart from other Asian cuisines.

Another key ingredient in Bhutanese cuisine is cheese, particularly the famous Bhutanese yak cheese. Yaks, which are native to the Himalayan region, are an integral part of Bhutanese culture, providing milk, meat, and wool. The cheese made from yak milk is a staple in Bhutanese households and is used in a variety of dishes, including soups, stews, and dumplings.

Bhutanese cuisine also celebrates the abundance of fresh vegetables and herbs found in the country's fertile valleys. From leafy greens like spinach and chard to root vegetables like potatoes and turnips, Bhutanese dishes are known for their colorful and nutritious ingredients. Traditional Bhutanese dishes often feature a mix of flavors, combining spicy, sour, and savory tastes to create a harmonious blend.

In this chapter, we will delve deeper into the traditions and techniques that make Bhutanese cuisine so unique. We will explore the culinary delights of Bhutanese festivals and cultural celebrations, the traditional methods of food preparation, and the sustainable practices that underpin Bhutanese agriculture. Join us as we uncover the secrets of Bhutanese cuisine and discover the flavors that have captivated the hearts and taste buds of travelers from around the world.

Exploring traditional Bhutanese dishes and cooking techniques

Bhutan, often referred to as the "Land of the Thunder Dragon," is a country steeped in rich cultural traditions, including its cuisine. For travelers eager to delve into the heart of Bhutanese culture, exploring traditional dishes and cooking techniques is a must.

Bhutanese cuisine is distinct and reflects the country's unique geography and indigenous ingredients. The Bhutanese people have mastered the art of using local produce to create flavorful and nourishing meals. With a strong emphasis on vegetables, grains, and spices, Bhutanese dishes are not only delicious but also healthy and sustainable.

One of the most popular Bhutanese dishes is "Ema Datshi," a spicy concoction made with chili peppers and cheese. This dish perfectly exemplifies the Bhutanese love for spicy food. Another staple is "Doma," a dish made from betel leaves filled with ingredients like dried fruits, nuts, and spices. It is often consumed after meals as a digestive aid.

The cooking techniques used in Bhutanese cuisine are rooted in tradition and are passed down through generations. One such technique is "pounding," where ingredients like chilies, cheese, and spices are pounded together using a mortar and pestle. This method allows the flavors to blend together harmoniously, resulting in a unique taste. Another technique is "fermentation," which is widely used in Bhutanese cuisine to enhance the flavors of various dishes.

For those interested in experiencing Bhutanese cuisine firsthand, there are ample opportunities to learn and participate in cooking classes. These classes offer a chance to engage with local chefs and learn about the significance of different ingredients, spices, and techniques. Through these classes, travelers can gain a deeper understanding of Bhutanese culture and the importance of food in the local way of life.

Exploring traditional Bhutanese dishes and cooking techniques is not only a culinary adventure but also a way to connect with the Bhutanese people on a deeper level. By immersing oneself in the flavors and traditions of Bhutan, travelers can gain a greater appreciation for the country's unique heritage and its pursuit of Gross National Happiness.

Whether you are a food enthusiast, a cultural explorer, or simply someone seeking a deeper connection with Bhutan, delving into the world of Bhutanese cuisine will undoubtedly be a memorable and fulfilling experience.

Learning about the importance of food in Bhutanese culture

Food plays a significant role in Bhutanese culture, reflecting its deep-rooted traditions and values. For travelers interested in exploring the rich cultural heritage of Bhutan, understanding the importance of food is essential. This subchapter delves into the significance of food in Bhutanese culture, offering insights into the country's culinary traditions, rituals, and beliefs.

Bhutanese spirituality and meditation practices are closely intertwined with the act of eating. In Bhutan, food is not merely sustenance but a means to nourish the body, mind, and spirit. The Bhutanese believe that the energy and intention put into preparing a meal directly affect its quality and the well-being of those who consume it. Travelers interested in Bhutanese spirituality can learn about the sacredness of food and the mindfulness associated with its consumption.

Bhutanese traditional arts and crafts also find expression in their culinary traditions. Intricate patterns and designs are often carved into wooden utensils and bowls used for food preparation and serving. These unique craft techniques highlight the importance of aesthetics and attention to detail in Bhutanese culture.

Furthermore, Bhutanese cuisine reflects the country's natural diversity and the availability of local produce. Traditional dishes such as Ema Datshi (chili and cheese stew) and Red Rice are not only delicious but also showcase Bhutan's agricultural practices and sustainable farming methods. Travelers interested in Bhutanese cuisine can explore the country's local markets, interact with farmers, and even participate in cooking classes to gain a deeper understanding of Bhutan's culinary heritage.

Food also plays a central role in Bhutanese festivals and cultural celebrations. Festivals like Tshechus are occasions for communities to come together and share meals. Traditional dishes are prepared in abundance, and the act of communal feasting symbolizes unity and harmony.

Exploring Bhutan's trekking and adventure tourism also offers opportunities to experience the country's biodiversity and wildlife conservation efforts. Travelers can witness the sustainable practices employed by local communities in cultivating organic food and preserving the fragile ecosystems that support Bhutan's unique flora and fauna.

In addition, Bhutanese traditional medicine and alternative healing practices often incorporate dietary recommendations. Learning about the medicinal properties of specific foods and the holistic approach to health and well-being can be a fascinating aspect for travelers interested in alternative healing practices.

Understanding Bhutanese architecture and traditional building techniques can provide insights into the design and construction of traditional kitchens and spaces dedicated to food preparation. These architectural marvels reflect the integration of cultural values and sustainable practices into daily life.

Lastly, Bhutanese textile and weaving traditions extend to the realm of food as well. Intricately woven tablecloths, aprons, and traditional attire worn during festivals add a touch of elegance to the dining experience, showcasing Bhutan's rich textile heritage.

By exploring the importance of food in Bhutanese culture, travelers can gain a deeper appreciation for the country's sustainable development and Gross National Happiness philosophy. Food serves as a gateway to understanding the interconnectedness of Bhutanese traditions, spirituality, arts, environment, and overall well-being.

Chapter 5: Bhutanese Festivals and Cultural Celebrations

Experiencing the vibrant festivals and celebrations in Bhutan

Bhutan, the Land of the Thunder Dragon, is a country known for its rich culture and vibrant traditions. One of the best ways to immerse yourself in the Bhutanese way of life is by participating in its numerous festivals and celebrations. These events not only showcase the country's unique heritage but also provide travelers with an unforgettable experience.

Bhutanese festivals are deeply rooted in spirituality, and they offer a glimpse into the country's rich religious traditions. One such festival is the Tsechu, an annual religious event held in various monasteries and dzongs throughout the country. During the Tsechu, locals and tourists alike gather to witness masked dances, vibrant costumes, and religious rituals performed by monks. It is believed that by attending these events, one can gain spiritual merit and blessings.

Apart from the religious festivals, Bhutan also celebrates cultural events that highlight the country's traditional arts and crafts. The Thimphu Tshechu, held in the capital city, showcases the finest examples of Bhutanese craftsmanship, including intricate paintings, woodwork, and sculptures. Visitors can witness artisans at work and even try their hand at some of these traditional crafts.

No visit to Bhutan is complete without indulging in its unique cuisine and culinary traditions. Bhutanese cuisine is known for its spicy flavors and use of locally sourced ingredients. Travelers can savor traditional dishes like Ema Datshi (chili and cheese stew) and Momos (dumplings) while learning about the importance of food in Bhutanese culture.

Bhutanese festivals are also an opportunity to explore the country's natural beauty. Many celebrations take place in picturesque locations, providing a backdrop of snow-capped mountains and lush valleys. Travelers can combine their festival experience with trekking and adventure tourism, exploring the breathtaking landscapes of Bhutan while immersing themselves in its vibrant culture.

In addition to its cultural heritage, Bhutan is also known for its commitment to biodiversity and wildlife conservation. Travelers can learn about Bhutanese conservation efforts by visiting national parks and participating in eco-tours. These experiences provide a deeper understanding of Bhutan's unique flora and fauna and the importance of preserving it for future generations.

For those seeking alternative healing practices, Bhutan offers traditional medicine and wellness retreats. Visitors can learn about the healing properties of local herbs and participate in meditation and mindfulness practices, gaining insights into Bhutanese spirituality and the pursuit of sustainable happiness.

The festivals and celebrations of Bhutan also provide an opportunity to marvel at the country's unique architecture and traditional building techniques. Dzongs, monasteries, and traditional Bhutanese houses showcase intricate woodwork and exquisite craftsmanship. Travelers can explore these architectural wonders and learn about the significance of design in Bhutanese culture.

Bhutanese textiles and weaving traditions are another highlight of the country's cultural heritage. Visitors can witness the intricate process of creating traditional Bhutanese garments and textiles. They can even try their hand at weaving, understanding the skill and dedication required to produce these beautiful works of art.

Lastly, experiencing Bhutan's festivals and celebrations provides insight into the country's pursuit of sustainable development and Gross National Happiness (GNH) philosophy. The emphasis on preserving culture, the environment, and the well-being of its citizens is evident in every aspect of Bhutanese life. By participating in these events, travelers can gain a deeper understanding of Bhutan's unique approach to happiness and well-being.

In conclusion, experiencing the vibrant festivals and celebrations in Bhutan is a must for travelers seeking an immersive cultural experience. From spiritual rituals and traditional arts to culinary delights and breathtaking landscapes, Bhutan offers a wealth of opportunities to explore its rich heritage and pursue sustainable happiness.

Understanding the significance of religious and cultural events

Religious and cultural events hold immense significance in Bhutanese society, and gaining a deeper understanding of these events can greatly enhance your travel experience in this enchanting Himalayan kingdom. From festivals to rituals, each event offers a unique insight into the spiritual, cultural, and historical fabric of Bhutan.

Bhutanese spirituality and meditation practices are deeply rooted in the country's Buddhist heritage. Exploring monasteries and meditation centers will allow you to witness the serene and contemplative lifestyle of Bhutanese monks and nuns. Engaging in meditation sessions can provide a glimpse into the Bhutanese approach to achieving inner peace and sustainable happiness.

Bhutanese traditional arts and crafts are a testament to the country's rich cultural heritage. From intricate paintings known as thangkas to delicate wood carvings and vibrant textiles, Bhutanese craftsmanship is renowned worldwide. Visiting art schools and workshops will give you a chance to witness the artistic skills passed down through generations and even try your hand at creating your own masterpiece.

Bhutanese cuisine and culinary traditions offer a tantalizing journey for your taste buds. From spicy chili cheese dishes to succulent momos (dumplings), Bhutanese cuisine is a delightful blend of flavors and textures. Exploring local markets, participating in cooking classes, and savoring traditional meals will provide a deeper understanding of Bhutanese culture through its culinary delights.

Bhutanese festivals and cultural celebrations are vibrant and colorful affairs that showcase the country's cultural richness. Witnessing festivals such as the famous Paro Tshechu or the Punakha Drubchen will immerse you in the joyous atmosphere of Bhutanese traditions, where masked dances, ancient rituals, and elaborate costumes take center stage.

Bhutanese trekking and adventure tourism offer thrilling experiences amidst the breathtaking landscapes of the country. Trekking through pristine valleys, ascending majestic peaks, and camping in remote regions will not only test your physical abilities but also expose you to the awe-inspiring beauty of Bhutan's nature and the deep spiritual connection its people have with the land.

Bhutanese biodiversity and wildlife conservation efforts are commendable, making it a haven for nature enthusiasts. Exploring national parks and engaging in eco-friendly activities will allow you to witness Bhutan's incredible flora and fauna, including the elusive snow leopard and the endangered black-necked crane.

Bhutanese traditional medicine and alternative healing practices offer unique insights into holistic healing methods. Visiting traditional medicine centers and learning about the use of medicinal plants and ancient healing techniques will shed light on Bhutan's approach to healthcare, which integrates body, mind, and spirit.

Bhutanese architecture and traditional building techniques present a fascinating blend of aesthetics and functionality. Exploring dzongs (fortresses), temples, and traditional houses will reveal the intricate details, vibrant colors, and the sustainable construction methods employed by Bhutanese artisans throughout history.

Bhutanese textile and weaving traditions are renowned for their intricate designs and vibrant colors. Visiting weaving centers and witnessing the skillful process of creating handwoven textiles will provide a deeper appreciation for the craftsmanship and cultural significance of Bhutanese textiles.

Lastly, understanding Bhutanese sustainable development and Gross National Happiness (GNH) philosophy is crucial to appreciate the unique approach Bhutan takes towards progress. Learning about GNH, which prioritizes holistic well-being and environmental conservation over material wealth, will inspire you to reflect on your own pursuit of sustainable happiness.

By immersing yourself in the significance of religious and cultural events in Bhutan, you will gain a profound appreciation for the country's spirituality, heritage, and commitment to sustainable development. Embrace the opportunity to delve into the heart and soul of Bhutan, and let the magic of its traditions and celebrations enrich your travel experience.

Participating in traditional dance and music performances

Participating in traditional dance and music performances in Bhutan is a captivating experience that allows travelers to immerse themselves in the rich cultural heritage of the country. Bhutanese dance and music are deeply rooted in spirituality and are an integral part of the Bhutanese way of life.

Bhutanese spirituality and meditation practices are known to promote inner peace and happiness. By participating in traditional dance and music performances, travelers can witness the spiritual essence that underlies these practices. The movements and rhythms of the dances are believed to channel divine energy and bring about a sense of tranquility. The music, often played using traditional instruments like the dramnyen and the lingm, creates a soothing ambiance that resonates with the soul.

Bhutanese traditional arts and crafts are renowned for their intricate designs and vibrant colors. Dance and music performances often feature traditional costumes and props, which are meticulously handcrafted by skilled artisans. By witnessing these performances, travelers can gain a deeper appreciation for the craftsmanship and artistic skills that go into creating these exquisite pieces.

Bhutanese cuisine and culinary traditions are an integral part of the country's culture. During dance and music performances, travelers have the opportunity to savor traditional Bhutanese dishes, which are often served as part of the celebrations. These culinary delights, such as ema datshi (chili and cheese stew) and momo (dumplings), provide a unique gastronomic experience that complements the cultural immersion.

Bhutanese festivals and cultural celebrations are vibrant and lively, filled with dance and music performances. By participating in these festivities, travelers can witness the joy and enthusiasm with which the Bhutanese people celebrate their traditions. The dances and music serve as a means of preserving and passing on the cultural heritage from one generation to another.

For adventure seekers, participating in traditional dance and music performances can be a thrilling experience. Many festivals and celebrations are held in remote locations, providing an opportunity for travelers to combine their love for trekking and adventure tourism with cultural immersion.

By engaging in traditional dance and music performances, travelers can also contribute to the preservation of Bhutanese biodiversity and wildlife conservation. Many dances depict animals and nature, highlighting the importance of protecting the environment.

Overall, participating in traditional dance and music performances in Bhutan offers travelers a unique and enriching experience. It allows them to delve into the spiritual, artistic, culinary, and cultural aspects of Bhutan, while also contributing to the preservation of its traditions and natural heritage.

Chapter 6: Bhutanese Trekking and Adventure Tourism

Overview of Bhutan's breathtaking landscapes and trekking routes

In the ethereal land of Bhutan, a hidden gem nestled in the heart of the Himalayas, nature's unparalleled beauty awaits the intrepid traveler. With its breathtaking landscapes and awe-inspiring trekking routes, Bhutan offers a truly unique experience for those seeking adventure, spirituality, and a deep connection with the natural world.

Bhutan's landscapes are nothing short of extraordinary. From snow-capped peaks to dense forests, cascading waterfalls to turquoise rivers, the country's diverse topography never fails to captivate the senses. The iconic Tiger's Nest Monastery, perched precariously on a cliffside, is a testament to the harmonious coexistence of man and nature in Bhutan. This sacred site is a pilgrimage destination for both locals and travelers alike, offering a profound spiritual experience amidst the stunning surroundings.

For those seeking an immersive journey into Bhutan's spirituality and meditation practices, the country's trekking routes provide the perfect opportunity. The mystical trails wind through serene valleys, passing ancient monasteries and meditation retreats where visitors can learn from enlightened masters. These treks offer a chance to explore Bhutan's rich spiritual heritage, fostering inner peace and tranquility in a truly enchanting setting.

Bhutan's traditional arts and crafts are another highlight of the country's cultural tapestry. Intricate paintings, woodwork, and sculptures showcase the craftsmanship and creativity of the Bhutanese people. Travelers can witness these ancient traditions come to life in the local workshops and interact with artisans who have honed their skills over generations.

No exploration of Bhutan would be complete without indulging in its unique culinary traditions. Bhutanese cuisine is a delightful blend of flavors, with traditional dishes like Ema Datshi (chili and cheese stew) and momos (dumplings) tantalizing the taste buds. Travelers can savor these authentic flavors while immersing themselves in the warm hospitality of the Bhutanese people.

Throughout the year, Bhutan comes alive with vibrant festivals and cultural celebrations. From the colorful Paro Tshechu to the masked dances of Punakha Dromchoe, these events offer a glimpse into the country's rich cultural heritage. Travelers can witness the joyous festivities, adorned in traditional attire, and partake in the lively dances and rituals that form an integral part of Bhutanese life.

For the adventure seekers, Bhutan's trekking and adventure tourism options are unparalleled. From the challenging Snowman Trek to the scenic Druk Path Trek, there are routes catering to all levels of fitness and experience. These treks take you through pristine landscapes, allowing you to witness the untamed beauty of Bhutan up close.

Bhutan's commitment to biodiversity and wildlife conservation is evident in its numerous protected areas. The country boasts a remarkable array of flora and fauna, including rare species like the takin and the black-necked crane. Conservation initiatives ensure the preservation of these natural treasures, offering travelers a chance to witness the wonders of Bhutan's wildlife in their natural habitats.

Bhutan's traditional medicine and alternative healing practices are deeply rooted in the country's cultural heritage. Travelers can explore the ancient healing techniques and therapies that have been passed down through generations. From herbal remedies to meditation practices, these traditions offer a holistic approach to wellness and rejuvenation.

Bhutan's architecture and traditional building techniques are a testament to the country's commitment to preserving its cultural identity. The intricately designed dzongs (fortresses) and monasteries showcase the architectural prowess of the Bhutanese people. Travelers can marvel at these masterpieces and gain insights into the techniques that have withstood the test of time.

Bhutan's textile and weaving traditions are renowned for their exquisite craftsmanship and vibrant colors. From intricately woven textiles to handcrafted garments, these traditional arts offer a window into Bhutan's rich cultural heritage. Travelers can witness the skillful weaving process and even try their hand at creating their own masterpiece.

At the heart of Bhutan's allure lies its philosophy of Gross National Happiness (GNH) and sustainable development. The country's commitment to preserving its unique cultural and natural heritage, while promoting the well-being of its people, is truly inspiring. Travelers can witness firsthand the harmony between nature, society, and the individual, making Bhutan a beacon of sustainable happiness.

In conclusion, Bhutan's breathtaking landscapes and trekking routes offer a gateway to a world of spirituality, adventure, and cultural immersion. Whether you seek the tranquility of meditation, the thrill of adventure, or the discovery of ancient traditions, Bhutan provides an unforgettable journey that will leave you with a profound sense of wonder and appreciation for the beauty of our planet.

Planning an adventure tour in Bhutan and necessary preparations

Bhutan, a small kingdom nestled in the Himalayas, is a paradise for adventure enthusiasts seeking a unique and culturally rich experience. With its commitment to sustainable development and the pursuit of

SUSTAINABLE HAPPINES: BHUTAN'S DEVELOPMENT
AND PURSUIT OF THE GROSS NATIONAL HAPPINESS   37

Gross National Happiness (GNH), Bhutan offers a variety of adventures that cater to different interests and abilities. Whether you are drawn to Bhutanese spirituality and meditation practices, traditional arts and crafts, culinary traditions, festivals, trekking, biodiversity and wildlife conservation, traditional medicine, architecture, textile and weaving traditions, or the GNH philosophy, planning your adventure tour in Bhutan requires careful consideration and necessary preparations.

Before embarking on your journey, it is crucial to research and understand the specific niche you are interested in exploring. Bhutanese spirituality and meditation practices offer a serene and introspective experience for travelers seeking inner peace and self-discovery. Various monasteries and meditation centers are scattered throughout the country, providing an opportunity to learn from experienced practitioners and immerse yourself in Bhutanese spiritual traditions.

For those interested in Bhutanese traditional arts and crafts, a visit to Thimphu, the capital city, is a must. The city houses numerous art studios and craft markets, where you can witness artisans creating intricate paintings, sculptures, and textiles. Engaging with these artists and learning about their techniques is a memorable way to appreciate Bhutan's rich artistic heritage.

No adventure tour is complete without indulging in the local cuisine and culinary traditions. Bhutanese cuisine is known for its spicy flavors and unique dishes like Ema Datshi (chili and cheese stew) and Momos (dumplings). Exploring the local markets and trying traditional Bhutanese delicacies is a delightful way to immerse yourself in the country's culinary culture.

Bhutanese festivals and cultural celebrations are a vibrant display of the country's rich heritage. Timing your adventure tour to coincide with festivals such as the Paro Tshechu or Thimphu Tshechu allows you to witness colorful mask dances, traditional music, and cultural performances. These celebrations offer a glimpse into Bhutan's deep-rooted traditions and provide an opportunity to connect with the local community.

For adventure seekers, Bhutan offers breathtaking trekking routes that traverse stunning landscapes, including the famous Snowman Trek and Jomolhari Trek. It is essential to prepare physically and mentally for these challenging treks and ensure you have the necessary equipment to navigate the rugged terrain.

Bhutan's commitment to biodiversity and wildlife conservation is evident in its extensive network of national parks and protected areas. Exploring these pristine habitats allows you to witness a diverse range of flora and fauna, including the elusive snow leopard and the endangered black-necked crane. Understanding and respecting the conservation efforts in place is crucial to ensure the sustainability of these ecosystems.

Bhutanese traditional medicine and alternative healing practices have been an integral part of the country's healthcare system for centuries. Exploring the traditional medicine centers and engaging with practitioners provides insights into Bhutan's holistic approach to well-being and alternative healing techniques.

The architecture and traditional building techniques of Bhutan are a testament to the country's commitment to preserving its cultural heritage. The iconic dzongs (fortresses) and monasteries showcase exquisite craftsmanship and serve as living examples of Bhutanese architectural traditions.

Bhutanese textile and weaving traditions are deeply rooted in the country's cultural identity. Visiting textile museums and weaving centers allows you to witness the intricate process of creating handwoven textiles, including the famous kira and gho garments.

Lastly, understanding Bhutan's sustainable development and GNH philosophy is essential for responsible travel. Bhutan's unique approach to development focuses on holistic well-being, environmental conservation, and cultural preservation. Embracing these principles and supporting local initiatives contribute to the sustainability and preservation of Bhutan's unique heritage.

In conclusion, planning an adventure tour in Bhutan requires careful consideration and necessary preparations. Whether you are interested in Bhutanese spirituality, traditional arts and crafts, culinary traditions, festivals, trekking, biodiversity conservation, traditional medicine, architecture, textiles, or the GNH philosophy, Bhutan offers a myriad of experiences to cater to your interests. By immersing yourself in Bhutan's rich cultural and natural heritage and embracing sustainable practices, you can embark on a transformative journey of self-discovery while contributing to the preservation and well-being of this enchanting kingdom.

Engaging in outdoor activities like hiking, biking, and rafting

Bhutan, with its pristine natural beauty and breathtaking landscapes, offers a wide range of outdoor activities for adventure enthusiasts. Whether you are a seasoned traveler or a nature lover, the kingdom of Bhutan has something to offer for everyone. From hiking through lush green forests to biking along scenic trails and rafting in crystal-clear rivers, exploring the outdoors in Bhutan is a truly exhilarating experience.

Hiking is one of the most popular outdoor activities in Bhutan. With its extensive network of trails, the country offers a plethora of options for all levels of hikers. Whether you want to embark on a challenging multi-day trek or opt for a leisurely day hike, Bhutan has it all. The famous Tiger's Nest hike, leading to the iconic Taktsang Monastery perched on a cliff, is a must-do for any traveler seeking a spiritual experience.

Biking in Bhutan is a fantastic way to explore the country's diverse landscapes and immerse yourself in its rich culture. From gentle rides through picturesque valleys to adrenaline-pumping downhill descents, Bhutan offers an array of biking trails suitable for all skill levels. As you pedal through quaint villages and verdant rice fields, you'll have the opportunity to interact with friendly locals and witness their traditional way of life.

For those seeking an adrenaline rush, rafting in Bhutan's pristine rivers is an experience not to be missed. The country boasts several rivers offering varying levels of difficulty for rafting enthusiasts. Whether you are a beginner or an experienced rafter, navigating through the rapids while surrounded by breathtaking scenery will leave you with memories to last a lifetime.

Engaging in these outdoor activities not only allows you to connect with nature but also provides a unique opportunity to immerse yourself in Bhutanese culture and traditions. The country's commitment to sustainable development and Gross National Happiness philosophy is reflected in its approach to adventure tourism. Bhutan ensures that these activities are conducted in an eco-friendly manner, preserving the delicate balance of its natural environment.

So, whether you are drawn to Bhutan for its spirituality, traditional arts and crafts, cuisine, or festivals, don't miss the chance to engage in outdoor activities like hiking, biking, and rafting. These experiences will not only leave you with a sense of fulfillment but also deepen your understanding of Bhutan's sustainable development and its pursuit of Gross National Happiness.

Chapter 7: Bhutanese Biodiversity and Wildlife Conservation

Discovering Bhutan's rich biodiversity and protected areas

Bhutan, a mystical kingdom nestled in the Himalayas, is not only known for its Gross National Happiness philosophy but also for its remarkable biodiversity and protected areas. For travelers seeking an unparalleled experience in nature and wildlife, Bhutan is a hidden gem waiting to be explored.

With its diverse range of ecosystems, Bhutan boasts a wealth of flora and fauna, making it one of the world's biodiversity hotspots. From lush subtropical forests to snow-capped peaks, the country is home to over 5,400 species of plants, including rare orchids and medicinal herbs used in traditional Bhutanese medicine.

Protected areas play a crucial role in conserving Bhutan's rich biodiversity. The country has established several national parks and wildlife sanctuaries, such as Jigme Dorji National Park and Phibsoo Wildlife Sanctuary, covering a significant portion of its land. These protected areas not only preserve the natural habitats of endangered species like the Bengal tiger and the black-necked crane but also provide travelers with the opportunity to witness them in their natural environment.

For nature enthusiasts, trekking through Bhutan's protected areas is a once-in-a-lifetime experience. The pristine landscapes, cascading waterfalls, and breathtaking vistas will leave you in awe. The Snowman Trek, renowned as one of the toughest treks in the world, takes you through remote villages, high mountain passes, and stunning alpine valleys, offering a chance to immerse yourself in the untouched beauty of Bhutan.

In addition to its abundant wildlife, Bhutan is also known for its unique cultural heritage. The Bhutanese people have a deep connection with nature, which is reflected in their spirituality and meditation practices. Travelers can participate in meditation retreats, guided by experienced monks, to find inner peace and gain a deeper understanding of Bhutanese spirituality.

Furthermore, Bhutanese traditional arts and crafts, such as thangka painting and wood carving, are integral to the country's cultural identity. Visitors can witness master artisans at work, preserving these ancient techniques and creating exquisite pieces that reflect Bhutan's natural surroundings.

To fully immerse yourself in Bhutan's rich biodiversity and protected areas, it is crucial to respect and support sustainable tourism practices. By choosing eco-friendly accommodations, engaging in responsible wildlife viewing, and supporting local conservation efforts, travelers can contribute to the preservation of this unique and fragile ecosystem.

Embark on a journey to Bhutan, where the pursuit of Gross National Happiness goes hand in hand with the preservation of its natural wonders. Discover the harmony between humans and nature, and experience the joy and fulfillment that comes from exploring a land teeming with biodiversity and protected areas.

Understanding the importance of wildlife conservation efforts

As travelers, we are often drawn to the beauty and wonder of the natural world. The breathtaking landscapes, the diverse flora and fauna, and the opportunity to witness the delicate balance of ecosystems in action are all reasons why we seek out destinations that offer a unique and authentic experience with nature. Bhutan, a country known for its commitment to sustainable development and Gross National Happiness (GNH) philosophy, is an ideal destination for those interested in wildlife conservation efforts.

Bhutanese spirituality and meditation practices have long been intertwined with the natural environment. The belief in the interconnectedness of all living beings and the importance of living in harmony with nature is deeply ingrained in Bhutanese culture. By understanding the importance of wildlife conservation, travelers can gain a deeper appreciation for the spiritual connection that Bhutanese people have with their environment.

Bhutanese traditional arts and crafts also reflect a deep respect for nature. The intricate designs and patterns found in Bhutanese textiles and weaving traditions often depict local wildlife and celebrate the biodiversity of the region. By supporting these traditional practices, travelers can contribute to the preservation of both cultural heritage and biodiversity.

Bhutanese cuisine and culinary traditions are heavily influenced by the country's rich natural resources. The use of locally sourced ingredients, many of which come from sustainable farming practices, ensures that the delicate balance of ecosystems is maintained. By experiencing Bhutanese cuisine, travelers can gain a greater understanding of the importance of conservation efforts and the role they play in preserving not only local flavors but also the habitats that support them.

Bhutanese festivals and cultural celebrations are another way to connect with the country's commitment to wildlife conservation. Many of these events pay homage to the natural world and its inhabitants, reminding us of the need to protect and preserve these precious resources.

For those seeking adventure, Bhutanese trekking and adventure tourism offer unique opportunities to explore the country's incredible biodiversity. From the snow-capped peaks of the Himalayas to the lush valleys and dense forests, Bhutan is teeming with a wide variety of wildlife. By engaging in responsible tourism practices, travelers can ensure that their presence has a positive impact on the environment and the local communities who depend on it.

In conclusion, understanding the importance of wildlife conservation efforts is essential for travelers interested in Bhutanese spirituality, traditional arts and crafts, cuisine, festivals, trekking, and adventure tourism. By supporting sustainable development and Gross National Happiness philosophy, we can contribute to the preservation of Bhutan's rich biodiversity and ensure that future generations can continue to enjoy the wonders of this unique and enchanting destination.

Participating in eco-friendly activities to support conservation

Bhutan, a tiny Himalayan kingdom known for its commitment to environmental preservation and sustainable development, offers travelers a unique opportunity to engage in eco-friendly activities that support conservation efforts. By actively participating in these activities, travelers can contribute to the preservation of Bhutan's rich natural and cultural heritage while experiencing the country's unique offerings.

One way to support conservation is by exploring Bhutan's vast biodiversity through guided nature walks and wildlife tours. Bhutan is home to a diverse range of flora and fauna, including rare and endangered species such as the snow leopard and the black-necked crane. By joining these tours, travelers not only get a chance to witness the beauty of Bhutan's natural landscapes but also contribute to the protection of these fragile ecosystems through their participation fees.

Another eco-friendly activity that travelers can engage in is volunteering for environmental restoration projects. Bhutan places great emphasis on the conservation of its forests, which are considered the country's "lungs." By participating in tree-planting initiatives and forest clean-up campaigns, travelers can directly contribute to the reforestation efforts and help preserve Bhutan's pristine landscapes for future generations.

Additionally, travelers can support conservation by opting for sustainable accommodations and eco-tourism practices. Bhutan has a range of eco-lodges that are built using traditional architectural techniques and operate with minimal environmental impact. By choosing to stay in these accommodations, travelers can experience traditional Bhutanese hospitality while minimizing their carbon footprint.

Engaging with local communities and learning about their traditional practices is another way to support conservation. Bhutanese spirituality and meditation practices, traditional arts and crafts, cuisine and culinary traditions, festivals, and cultural celebrations are all deeply intertwined with the country's natural surroundings. By participating in workshops and interacting with local artisans, chefs, and monks, travelers can not only gain insights into Bhutanese traditions but also contribute to the preservation of these cultural practices.

In conclusion, participating in eco-friendly activities to support conservation enables travelers to have a meaningful and sustainable travel experience in Bhutan. By actively engaging in these activities, travelers can contribute to the preservation of Bhutan's natural and cultural heritage, support local communities, and help create a more sustainable future.

Chapter 8: Bhutanese Traditional Medicine and Alternative Healing Practices

Exploring the principles of Bhutanese traditional medicine

Bhutan, a small kingdom nestled in the Eastern Himalayas, is not only famous for its stunning landscapes and Gross National Happiness philosophy but also for its rich tradition of holistic healthcare. The principles of Bhutanese traditional medicine, also known as Sowa Rigpa, have been passed down through generations and continue to play a significant role in the lives of Bhutanese people.

Rooted in Buddhist philosophy and influenced by Tibetan and Indian Ayurvedic traditions, Bhutanese traditional medicine is based on the belief that the body, mind, and spirit are interconnected. It emphasizes the balance between these elements to achieve optimal health and well-being. Travelers interested in holistic healing and alternative therapies will find Bhutanese traditional medicine fascinating and enlightening.

The core principles of Bhutanese traditional medicine revolve around the concept of three humors or energies – Wind, Bile, and Phlegm. These energies are believed to govern the functioning of the body and maintaining their equilibrium is crucial for good health. Bhutanese traditional medicine practitioners diagnose and treat ailments by assessing the balance of these humors through various methods, including pulse reading, urine examination, and questioning.

Herbal medicine plays a central role in Bhutanese traditional medicine. The country's diverse ecosystems provide a wealth of medicinal plants, and traditional healers use their knowledge to create unique formulations for different ailments. These herbal remedies are often combined with dietary and lifestyle recommendations, physical therapies, and spiritual practices to promote holistic healing.

In addition to herbal medicine, Bhutanese traditional medicine also incorporates other modalities such as acupuncture, moxibustion, cupping, and external therapies like hot stone baths and oil massages. These practices aim to restore balance, remove blockages, and enhance the body's natural healing abilities.

Exploring the principles of Bhutanese traditional medicine offers a profound insight into the country's cultural heritage and its deep connection with nature. It is a testament to the Bhutanese people's commitment to holistic wellness and their sustainable way of life.

Travelers interested in Bhutanese spirituality, meditation practices, and alternative healing methods will find the principles of Bhutanese traditional medicine particularly intriguing. By embracing these principles, one can gain a deeper understanding of Bhutan's unique approach to well-being and its efforts to promote sustainable happiness.

Whether you are seeking to learn more about holistic healthcare, experience alternative therapies, or simply appreciate Bhutan's rich cultural heritage, exploring the principles of Bhutanese traditional medicine is a must for any traveler on the path to self-discovery and wellness.

Learning about herbal remedies and healing techniques

Learning about herbal remedies and healing techniques is an essential part of understanding Bhutanese traditional medicine and alternative healing practices. This subchapter aims to introduce travelers to the rich heritage of herbal remedies and healing techniques that have been passed down through generations in Bhutan.

Bhutanese traditional medicine, known as Sowa Rigpa, is an ancient healing system that combines herbal medicine, diet, meditation, and external therapies to restore balance and harmony in the body. It is rooted in the belief that physical ailments are often a manifestation of imbalances in the mind and spirit.

Travelers interested in Bhutanese spirituality and meditation practices will find that learning about herbal remedies and healing techniques is closely intertwined with these practices. Many of the herbs used in traditional medicine are also used for spiritual purposes, such as purifying the mind and enhancing meditation practices. By exploring these herbal remedies, travelers can gain a deeper understanding of the holistic approach to healing in Bhutan.

Furthermore, learning about herbal remedies and healing techniques provides insights into Bhutanese biodiversity and wildlife conservation efforts. Bhutan is known for its diverse flora and fauna, and many of the medicinal plants used in traditional medicine are sourced from the country's rich natural resources. By understanding the importance of these plants in healing practices, travelers can develop a greater appreciation for Bhutan's commitment to preserving its natural heritage.

In addition to the medicinal properties of herbs, this subchapter also delves into Bhutanese traditional arts and crafts related to herbal remedies. Bhutanese artisans have mastered the art of creating beautiful and intricate traditional medicine packaging, incense, and other herbal products. This subchapter explores the various techniques and materials used in these crafts, giving travelers a glimpse into the skilled craftsmanship that goes into producing these traditional healing products.

Whether travelers are interested in Bhutanese spirituality, traditional arts and crafts, or sustainable development and Gross National Happiness philosophy, learning about herbal remedies and healing techniques is an enriching experience. By delving into this subchapter, travelers can gain a deeper understanding of Bhutan's cultural heritage and the integral role of herbal remedies and healing techniques in the pursuit of sustainable happiness.

Experiencing alternative healing practices like acupuncture and meditation

In the pursuit of sustainable happiness, it is important to explore alternative healing practices that can bring balance and well-being to our lives. Bhutan, a country known for its commitment to Gross National Happiness (GNH), offers a unique opportunity for travelers to experience ancient healing techniques such as acupuncture and meditation.

Acupuncture, an ancient Chinese practice, involves the insertion of thin needles into specific points on the body to stimulate energy flow and promote healing. In Bhutan, acupuncture is not only used as a medical treatment but also as a way to achieve spiritual harmony. Travelers can visit traditional clinics and experience acupuncture sessions guided by experienced practitioners who integrate Bhutanese spirituality and meditation practices into their treatments. This holistic approach allows for a deeper connection between the mind, body, and spirit, promoting overall well-being and happiness.

Meditation is another powerful practice that has been embraced by the Bhutanese people for centuries. The serene landscapes of Bhutan provide the perfect backdrop for travelers to engage in meditation and mindfulness practices. From tranquil monasteries to secluded mountain retreats, there are numerous opportunities for visitors to learn meditation techniques and experience the transformative power of stillness and self-reflection.

By engaging in these alternative healing practices, travelers can not only improve their own well-being but also gain a deeper understanding of Bhutanese spirituality and meditation practices. These practices are deeply rooted in the country's cultural and religious traditions, and by participating in them, travelers can gain a profound insight into the Bhutanese way of life.

In addition to acupuncture and meditation, travelers can also explore other alternative healing practices in Bhutan, such as traditional medicine and herbal remedies. Bhutanese traditional medicine, known as Sowa Rigpa, is a holistic approach that combines herbal medicine, diet, meditation, and other therapies to restore balance and promote healing. Visitors can visit traditional medicine clinics, where experienced doctors prescribe personalized treatments based on the principles of Sowa Rigpa.

Overall, experiencing alternative healing practices like acupuncture and meditation in Bhutan offers travelers a unique opportunity to immerse themselves in the country's rich cultural heritage and spiritual traditions. By embracing these practices, visitors can cultivate a deeper sense of well-being, contributing to their own sustainable happiness and fostering a greater understanding of Bhutanese spirituality and the pursuit of Gross National Happiness.

Chapter 9: Bhutanese Architecture and Traditional Building Techniques

Appreciating the unique architectural style of Bhutanese buildings

As travelers embark on a journey through the enchanting kingdom of Bhutan, they are immediately struck by the distinctive architectural style that graces the landscape. Bhutanese buildings, with their intricate designs, vibrant colors, and integration with nature, are a testament to the country's rich cultural heritage and commitment to sustainable development.

Bhutanese spirituality and meditation practices have greatly influenced the architectural style of the country. The buildings, whether monasteries, temples, or even humble homes, are designed to create a harmonious space that promotes inner peace and tranquility. The use of sacred geometry, such as the mandala, and intricate wood carvings depict Buddhist teachings and serve as a visual reminder of the spiritual path.

Traditional arts and crafts play a significant role in Bhutanese architecture. Skilled artisans employ age-old techniques to create stunning details on the buildings, from hand-carved wooden beams to intricate paintings on the walls. These artistic expressions not only beautify the structures but also preserve and pass down Bhutanese cultural traditions to future generations.

Bhutanese cuisine and culinary traditions are also reflected in the architecture. Many traditional buildings feature large kitchens, as food holds great importance in Bhutanese culture. The seamless integration of kitchens into the design ensures that the aroma of delicious Bhutanese dishes wafts through the air, evoking a sense of warmth and hospitality.

Bhutanese festivals and cultural celebrations bring communities together and inspire the architecture of the country. During these festive occasions, buildings are adorned with vibrant colors and intricate decorations, showcasing the joy and exuberance that permeates Bhutanese society. The architecture becomes a canvas for cultural expression, creating a visual feast for the eyes.

Bhutanese trekking and adventure tourism also have an impact on the architectural style. Many remote monasteries and hermitages are built on high mountain passes or nestled in secluded valleys, offering breathtaking views and a sense of serenity. The strategic placement of these buildings allows travelers to experience the awe-inspiring beauty of Bhutan's landscape while immersing themselves in its spiritual essence.

Bhutanese architecture and traditional building techniques demonstrate a deep connection with the natural environment. The use of locally sourced materials, such as stone and rammed earth, ensures that the buildings blend seamlessly with the surrounding landscape. The incorporation of elements like courtyards, verandas, and traditional Bhutanese windows allows for natural light and ventilation, minimizing the need for artificial resources.

Bhutanese textile and weaving traditions find expression in the architecture as well. Colorful fabrics and intricate patterns adorn the interior spaces, adding a touch of vibrancy and elegance. The use of textiles also serves practical purposes, providing insulation during the harsh winters and enhancing the overall comfort of the buildings.

Bhutanese architecture is a testament to the country's commitment to sustainable development and the Gross National Happiness (GNH) philosophy. Buildings are designed to be environmentally friendly, incorporating renewable energy sources and utilizing passive design principles. The architectural style promotes a holistic approach to development, ensuring the well-being of both the people and the environment.

In conclusion, the unique architectural style of Bhutanese buildings is a reflection of the country's spirituality, cultural traditions, and sustainable development practices. Travelers who appreciate Bhutanese spirituality, traditional arts, culinary delights, festivals, adventure tourism, biodiversity, traditional medicine, textile traditions, and the pursuit of happiness will be captivated by the architectural wonders that grace the kingdom. Bhutan's buildings are not merely structures; they are living testaments to the country's rich cultural heritage and its harmonious coexistence with the natural world.

Understanding the use of traditional materials and techniques

In the enchanting kingdom of Bhutan, the preservation of traditional materials and techniques plays a crucial role in maintaining the country's unique cultural heritage and promoting sustainable development. This subchapter aims to provide travelers with insights into the significance of traditional materials and techniques in different aspects of Bhutanese life, including spirituality, arts and crafts, cuisine, festivals, trekking, biodiversity conservation, traditional medicine, architecture, textile, and sustainable development.

Bhutanese Spirituality and Meditation Practices:

Traditional materials and techniques are deeply intertwined with spirituality and meditation practices in Bhutan. The use of natural materials like wood, stone, and clay in the construction of monasteries and meditation retreats provides a serene and harmonious environment for spiritual seekers.

Bhutanese Traditional Arts and Crafts:

The vibrant tradition of Bhutanese arts and crafts relies heavily on traditional materials and techniques. Skilled artisans use bamboo, wood, clay, and natural dyes to create intricate paintings, sculptures, and textiles, reflecting the rich cultural heritage of the country.

Bhutanese Cuisine and Culinary Traditions:

Traditional materials and techniques are vital in the preparation of Bhutanese cuisine. The use of traditional earthenware pots and wood-fired ovens enhances the flavors of local ingredients, while traditional cooking techniques, such as fermenting and drying, preserve food for longer periods.

Bhutanese Festivals and Cultural Celebrations:

Traditional materials and techniques are prominently displayed during Bhutanese festivals and cultural celebrations. Elaborate costumes made from handwoven textiles and traditional masks crafted from wood and clay are used to depict mythical characters, adding a touch of mysticism to these vibrant events.

Bhutanese Trekking and Adventure Tourism:

Exploring Bhutan's breathtaking landscapes and trekking trails allows travelers to witness the traditional building techniques employed in constructing trails, bridges, and shelters. The use of local materials like stone and timber ensures minimal impact on the environment.

Bhutanese Biodiversity and Wildlife Conservation:

Traditional materials and techniques are instrumental in Bhutan's efforts to conserve its rich biodiversity. Sustainable practices, such as using traditional building techniques and materials in constructing eco-friendly lodges and wildlife viewing platforms, help maintain the delicate balance between development and conservation.

Bhutanese Traditional Medicine and Alternative Healing Practices:

Traditional materials and techniques are integral to Bhutanese traditional medicine and alternative healing practices. Medicinal herbs, minerals, and other natural ingredients are used in conjunction with traditional methods like moxibustion and hot stone therapy to promote health and wellbeing.

Bhutanese Architecture and Traditional Building Techniques:

The architecture of Bhutan reflects the country's deep-rooted traditions and respect for the environment. Traditional building techniques, such as rammed earth construction, utilize locally available materials to create durable and energy-efficient structures that blend seamlessly with the natural surroundings.

Bhutanese Textile and Weaving Traditions:

Bhutanese textiles are renowned for their intricate designs and vibrant colors. Traditional weaving techniques passed down through generations are used to create exquisite fabrics, using natural dyes derived from plants and traditional looms.

Bhutanese Sustainable Development and Gross National Happiness (GNH) Philosophy:

The use of traditional materials and techniques is at the core of Bhutan's sustainable development and GNH philosophy. By embracing traditional practices, Bhutan promotes cultural preservation, environmental conservation, and the overall wellbeing of its citizens, leading to sustainable happiness.

In conclusion, understanding the use of traditional materials and techniques in Bhutan provides travelers with a deeper appreciation for the country's spirituality, arts and crafts, cuisine, festivals, trekking, biodiversity conservation, traditional medicine, architecture, textile, and sustainable development. By immersing themselves in the rich cultural heritage of Bhutan, travelers can contribute to the preservation of this unique kingdom and experience the true essence of sustainable happiness.

Visiting monasteries, dzongs, and traditional houses

Visiting monasteries, dzongs, and traditional houses in Bhutan offers travelers a fascinating insight into the country's rich cultural heritage and spiritual traditions. Bhutan, known as the Land of the Thunder Dragon, is a deeply spiritual and mystical place where happiness is considered a measure of success. As you explore the country, you will be captivated by the serene beauty of its monasteries, dzongs, and traditional houses.

Monasteries, or gompas, are at the heart of Bhutanese spirituality and meditation practices. These ancient structures are perched high on mountain slopes, providing breathtaking views and a tranquil environment for meditation and contemplation. Visitors are welcome to observe the monks in prayer and experience the profound sense of peace that permeates these sacred spaces.

Dzongs are another architectural marvel that you must not miss. These fortified structures serve as both administrative centers and monastic institutions. Built without the use of nails, dzongs are symbolic of Bhutanese traditional arts and crafts and are a testament to the country's rich architectural heritage. Inside, you'll find beautifully painted murals, intricate woodwork, and stunning Buddhist statues.

For those interested in Bhutanese cuisine and culinary traditions, a visit to a traditional house is a must. Bhutanese food is a unique blend of flavors, with the famous Ema Datshi (chili and cheese) being a favorite among locals. Traditional houses offer an opportunity to learn about the art of Bhutanese cooking and try your hand at preparing a traditional meal.

Bhutanese festivals and cultural celebrations are an integral part of the country's social fabric. These vibrant and colorful events offer a glimpse into the Bhutanese way of life and their deep-rooted beliefs. From the lively Tshechus with their masked dances to the sacred rituals of the Wangdue Phodrang festival, experiencing these cultural celebrations will leave you in awe of Bhutan's rich cultural heritage.

For adventure enthusiasts, Bhutan offers a plethora of trekking and adventure tourism opportunities. From hiking through pristine forests to conquering towering peaks, the country's diverse landscapes provide a playground for outdoor enthusiasts. Embark on a trek to the famous Tiger's Nest, a cliffside monastery that offers breathtaking views and a spiritual experience like no other.

Bhutan's commitment to biodiversity and wildlife conservation is commendable. The country is home to rare and endangered species such as the snow leopard, takin, and black-necked crane. Explore the protected areas and national parks to witness the diverse fauna and flora that thrive in Bhutan's pristine environment.

Traditional medicine and alternative healing practices are deeply rooted in Bhutanese culture. Discover the ancient art of healing through herbal remedies and traditional therapies, which have been passed down through generations. Visit traditional medicine clinics and learn about the holistic approach to healthcare that is an integral part of Bhutanese society.

Bhutanese architecture and traditional building techniques reflect the country's respect for nature and its sustainable development principles. Traditional buildings are constructed using locally sourced materials and techniques that have been perfected over centuries. Learn about the intricate woodwork, colorful paintings, and the unique architectural style that makes Bhutanese buildings truly exceptional.

Bhutan's textile and weaving traditions are renowned for their intricate designs and vibrant colors. Explore local weaving centers and witness the skill and dedication of Bhutanese weavers as they create beautiful textiles using traditional techniques. From intricately patterned kiras to colorful hand-woven carpets, Bhutan's textile industry is a testament to the country's commitment to preserving its cultural heritage.

Lastly, a visit to Bhutan offers a unique opportunity to understand the concept of Gross National Happiness (GNH) and sustainable development. Bhutan's focus on well-being, environmental conservation, and cultural preservation sets it apart from other nations. Immerse yourself in the philosophy of GNH and discover the true meaning of sustainable happiness.

In summary, visiting monasteries, dzongs, and traditional houses in Bhutan provides an immersive experience into the country's spirituality, cultural heritage, and sustainable development principles. Whether you're interested in meditation practices, traditional arts and crafts, cuisine, festivals, adventure tourism, biodiversity, traditional medicine, architecture, textiles, or Gross National Happiness, Bhutan has something to offer every traveler seeking a unique and meaningful experience.

Chapter 10: Bhutanese Textile and Weaving Traditions

Introduction to Bhutanese textile and weaving heritage

Bhutan, a small landlocked country nestled in the heart of the Himalayas, is not only known for its breathtaking landscapes and Gross National Happiness philosophy but also for its rich textile and weaving heritage. For centuries, the Bhutanese people have perfected the art of creating intricate textiles, which reflect their deep cultural and spiritual traditions.

Weaving in Bhutan is more than just a craft; it is a way of life deeply intertwined with the country's identity. Each region in Bhutan has its unique weaving techniques, patterns, and designs, making it a fascinating journey to explore the diverse textile traditions across the country.

The Bhutanese people believe that weaving is not just a means of creating beautiful fabrics but also a spiritual practice. It is believed that the colors, patterns, and symbols used in the textiles have the power to bring harmony and balance to the wearer and the environment. The intricate patterns often depict Buddhist symbols, auspicious motifs, and elements of nature, reflecting the deep connection between Bhutanese spirituality and the art of weaving.

One of the most famous textile traditions in Bhutan is the Kira and Gho, the national dress for women and men, respectively. The Kira is a long, rectangular cloth worn by women, while the Gho is a knee-length robe worn by men. These garments are woven with great precision and skill, using traditional backstrap looms or treadle looms. The intricate patterns and vibrant colors of the Kira and Gho showcase the remarkable craftsmanship of Bhutanese weavers.

In addition to clothing, Bhutanese textiles are also used for various purposes, including ceremonial offerings, religious rituals, and home decor. The intricate hand-woven fabrics are transformed into wall hangings, table runners, rugs, and even prayer flags. Each piece of textile tells a story, preserving the cultural heritage and traditions of Bhutan.

Visitors to Bhutan have the opportunity to witness the art of weaving firsthand. Many villages across the country have weaving centers where skilled artisans demonstrate the entire process, from spinning yarn to creating complex patterns. Travelers can also try their hand at weaving, learning the ancient techniques and experiencing the meditative qualities of this traditional craft.

Exploring Bhutan's textile and weaving heritage is not only an opportunity to appreciate the artistic skills of the Bhutanese people but also a way to support sustainable development and cultural preservation. By purchasing authentic Bhutanese textiles, travelers can contribute to the livelihoods of local weavers and help ensure the continuation of this precious tradition for future generations.

In the chapters that follow, we delve deeper into the various aspects of Bhutanese textile and weaving traditions, exploring the techniques, symbolism, and cultural significance behind these beautiful creations. Join us on this journey to discover the vibrant world of Bhutanese textiles and experience the magic they hold.

Learning about the different types of Bhutanese textiles

Bhutanese textiles hold a significant place in the country's rich cultural heritage. They are not just pieces of fabric; they are an expression of Bhutanese identity, tradition, and artistry. Exploring the world of Bhutanese textiles is a fascinating journey that unveils the various types, techniques, and symbolism behind these intricate creations.

One of the most famous types of Bhutanese textiles is the kira and gho, which are the traditional attire for Bhutanese women and men, respectively. Kiras are woven from fine silk and adorned with intricate patterns and vibrant colors. Each region in Bhutan has its own unique weaving style, motifs, and designs, reflecting the diverse cultural heritage of the country.

Another type of Bhutanese textile is the thagzo, a handwoven brocade used for ceremonial purposes. Thagzo fabrics are often used to make religious garments, such as the kabney (a ceremonial scarf) and the rachu (a decorative belt). These textiles are intricately woven with gold and silver threads, creating exquisite patterns and designs that hold deep spiritual significance.

Bhutanese textiles also include the famous yathra, a handwoven woolen fabric. Yathras are known for their bold patterns and vibrant colors, often depicting Bhutanese motifs like dragons, flowers, and geometric designs. They are commonly used for making blankets, rugs, and bags, and are highly valued for their warmth and durability.

Learning about Bhutanese textiles is not just about understanding the different types; it is also about appreciating the traditional weaving techniques passed down through generations. Bhutanese weavers use backstrap looms, a traditional method that involves tying one end of the loom to a stationary object and the other end to the weaver's body. This method allows for precision and control, resulting in finely crafted textiles.

Bhutanese textiles are not just beautiful pieces of art; they also represent the country's commitment to sustainable development and preserving its cultural heritage. Many weavers in Bhutan practice sustainable techniques, using natural dyes made from plants and herbs. This not only protects the environment but also ensures the longevity of traditional weaving practices.

For travelers interested in Bhutanese spirituality, meditation practices, and traditional arts and crafts, exploring the world of Bhutanese textiles is a must. It offers a glimpse into the country's unique cultural traditions, its commitment to sustainable development, and its pursuit of Gross National Happiness. By supporting local weavers and learning about their craft, travelers can contribute to the preservation of Bhutan's vibrant textile heritage and promote sustainable tourism practices.

Participating in weaving workshops and supporting local artisans

Bhutan is a country renowned for its rich cultural heritage and traditional arts and crafts. One such craft that holds great significance in Bhutanese culture is weaving. Weaving in Bhutan is not just a means of producing fabrics, but it is also an art form that is deeply rooted in the country's history and spirituality. By participating in weaving workshops and supporting local artisans, travelers can not only learn about this ancient craft but also contribute to the preservation of Bhutanese cultural traditions.

Weaving workshops provide a unique opportunity for travelers to gain hands-on experience in the intricate process of weaving. Under the guidance of skilled Bhutanese weavers, participants can learn about the various weaving techniques, patterns, and designs that have been passed down through generations. These workshops are not only informative but also therapeutic, as the rhythmic movements of the loom can be a meditative experience, allowing participants to experience a sense of mindfulness and tranquility.

By supporting local artisans through purchasing their handcrafted textiles, travelers can directly contribute to the sustainability of Bhutanese traditional arts and crafts. Each woven piece tells a story, reflecting the cultural identity and spirituality of the Bhutanese people. By owning these textiles, travelers can bring a piece of Bhutan's rich heritage back home, creating a lasting connection to the country and its people.

Moreover, participating in weaving workshops and supporting local artisans aligns with Bhutan's philosophy of Gross National Happiness (GNH) and sustainable development. Bhutan places great importance on preserving its cultural traditions and ensuring the well-being of its citizens. By investing in local craftsmanship, travelers are directly supporting the livelihoods of artisans and contributing to the overall happiness and well-being of the Bhutanese people.

In conclusion, participating in weaving workshops and supporting local artisans provides travelers with a unique opportunity to immerse themselves in Bhutanese culture and contribute to the preservation of its rich heritage. By engaging in this traditional art form, travelers can not only learn about Bhutan's weaving traditions but also experience a sense of mindfulness and tranquility. Additionally, supporting local artisans through purchasing their handcrafted textiles aligns with Bhutan's philosophy of Gross National Happiness and sustainable development. So, whether you are a traveler interested in Bhutanese spirituality, traditional arts and crafts, or sustainable development, participating in weaving workshops and supporting local artisans is a must-do experience during your visit to Bhutan.

Chapter 11: Bhutanese Sustainable Development and Gross National Happiness (GNH) Philosophy

Exploring Bhutan's approach to sustainable development

In the pursuit of Gross National Happiness (GNH), Bhutan has gained international recognition for its unique approach to sustainable development. This small Himalayan kingdom has placed the well-being of its people and the preservation of its rich cultural heritage and environment at the center of its development policies.

Bhutan's commitment to sustainable development is deeply rooted in its spiritual and meditation practices. The country is known for its emphasis on mindfulness and inner peace, which are integral to Bhutanese spirituality. Travelers can immerse themselves in this ancient wisdom by participating in meditation retreats and learning from revered Buddhist masters.

Bhutan's traditional arts and crafts also reflect its sustainable development philosophy. The intricate woodwork, painting, and sculpture that can be seen in monasteries and dzongs (fortresses) are made using traditional techniques passed down through generations. Travelers can witness the creativity and skill of Bhutanese artisans by visiting craft centers and attending workshops.

No exploration of Bhutan is complete without indulging in its culinary traditions. Bhutanese cuisine is known for its unique flavors, with dishes often incorporating locally grown organic ingredients. Travelers can savor the taste of Bhutan by trying dishes like ema datshi (cheese and chili), momos (dumplings), and red rice, all prepared using sustainable farming practices.

Bhutanese festivals and cultural celebrations offer travelers a glimpse into the country's vibrant traditions. These events, such as the Paro Tshechu and Thimphu Tshechu, showcase colorful costumes, mask dances, and traditional music. By participating in these festivities, travelers can immerse themselves in the cultural heritage that Bhutan is working tirelessly to preserve.

For adventure enthusiasts, Bhutan offers breathtaking trekking and adventure tourism opportunities. The country's pristine landscapes, including the famous Tiger's Nest monastery, provide the perfect backdrop for outdoor activities. Bhutan's commitment to sustainable tourism ensures that these activities are carried out responsibly, minimizing the impact on the environment.

Bhutan's commitment to biodiversity and wildlife conservation is evident in its vast protected areas and national parks. Travelers can explore these natural wonders, home to endangered species such as the snow leopard and red panda. Bhutan's dedication to preserving its rich biodiversity ensures that future generations can enjoy these natural treasures.

Additionally, Bhutanese traditional medicine and alternative healing practices are gaining recognition for their holistic approach to well-being. Travelers can learn about these ancient healing techniques by visiting traditional medicine centers and experiencing treatments like hot stone baths and herbal therapies.

Bhutan's architecture and traditional building techniques reflect its commitment to sustainable development. The country's unique dzongs and traditional houses are built using locally sourced materials and designed to harmonize with the natural surroundings. Travelers can appreciate the beauty of Bhutanese architecture by exploring these ancient structures.

Finally, Bhutan's textile and weaving traditions showcase the country's rich cultural heritage. Travelers can witness the intricate art of weaving by visiting textile museums and observing weavers at work. Bhutanese textiles are known for their vibrant colors and intricate patterns, making them cherished souvenirs for visitors.

Exploring Bhutan's approach to sustainable development offers travelers a unique and enriching experience. From immersing in Bhutanese spirituality to indulging in its cuisine, trekking through its pristine landscapes, and witnessing its vibrant festivals, every aspect of Bhutan's sustainable development journey is an invitation to discover a harmonious way of life. As travelers engage with Bhutan's philosophy of Gross National Happiness, they become part of an extraordinary endeavor to create a sustainable and happy future for all.

Understanding the four pillars of Gross National Happiness

In the pursuit of happiness, Bhutan has taken a unique approach by measuring its progress through a holistic framework known as Gross National Happiness (GNH). This philosophy, rooted in Bhutanese culture and spirituality, emphasizes the well-being of individuals, communities, and the environment. To truly understand Bhutan and its commitment to sustainable happiness, it is essential to grasp the four pillars that form the foundation of GNH.

The first pillar is sustainable and equitable socio-economic development. Bhutan recognizes that material wealth alone does not equate to happiness. Instead, it strives for a balanced approach that ensures the well-being of all citizens, aiming to eradicate poverty, reduce inequality, and promote sustainable livelihoods. Visitors to Bhutan can witness this commitment through initiatives such as community-based homestays and fair-trade crafts, which empower local communities and contribute to their socio-economic development.

The second pillar is preservation and promotion of Bhutanese culture. Bhutan takes immense pride in its distinct cultural heritage, and it is deeply intertwined with the pursuit of happiness. From traditional arts and crafts to culinary traditions, festivals, and celebrations, Bhutanese culture is a vibrant tapestry that reflects the values and spirituality of the people. Travelers can immerse themselves in this rich cultural tapestry by participating in festivals, visiting monasteries, and exploring the country's unique architecture and building techniques.

The third pillar is environmental conservation. Bhutan is often referred to as the "last Shangri-La," and for good reason. Its pristine landscapes, lush forests, and diverse wildlife are a testament to the country's commitment to environmental preservation. Bhutan has set aside more than 50% of its land under protected areas, ensuring the conservation of its biodiversity. Travelers can experience this firsthand by engaging in eco-friendly trekking and adventure tourism activities, witnessing the country's breathtaking natural beauty while leaving a minimal ecological footprint.

The fourth pillar is good governance. Bhutan recognizes that effective governance is essential for fostering happiness and well-being. The country's democratic system, guided by the principles of GNH, ensures that decision-making considers the long-term well-being of its citizens and the environment. Visitors can gain insights into Bhutan's governance system by exploring its sustainable development practices and engaging with local communities.

Understanding the four pillars of Gross National Happiness provides a glimpse into the unique philosophy that shapes Bhutan's sustainable development. It offers travelers an opportunity to immerse themselves in Bhutanese spirituality, arts and crafts, culinary traditions, festivals, trekking adventures, biodiversity, traditional medicine, architecture, and textile traditions. By embracing GNH, Bhutan has created a society that values the happiness and well-being of its people and the preservation of its unique culture and environment.

Examining the impact of GNH on Bhutanese society and economy

Bhutan, a small Himalayan kingdom nestled between India and China, has long been an enigma to the outside world. With its unique approach to development, centered around the philosophy of Gross National Happiness (GNH), Bhutan has been able to create a society and economy that prioritizes the well-being of its people and the preservation of its culture and environment.

One of the key areas where the impact of GNH can be seen is in Bhutanese society. The emphasis on happiness and well-being has led to a society that values community, compassion, and spiritual growth. Bhutanese spirituality and meditation practices have thrived under the GNH framework, with many travelers coming to the country to learn from the masters and experience the transformative power of mindfulness and self-reflection.

The preservation of Bhutanese traditional arts and crafts is another area where GNH has made a significant impact. The government has actively supported artisans and craftsmen, encouraging the continuation of traditional techniques and the production of high-quality, handmade products. Travelers with an interest in Bhutanese traditional arts can explore local workshops and markets, where they can witness the skill and creativity of Bhutanese artisans firsthand.

Bhutanese cuisine and culinary traditions have also flourished under the GNH philosophy. With an emphasis on organic farming and the use of local ingredients, Bhutanese cuisine is not only delicious but also sustainable. Travelers can indulge in dishes like ema datshi (chili and cheese), momo (dumplings), and suja (butter tea), while also supporting local farmers and promoting food security.

Bhutanese festivals and cultural celebrations are an integral part of the country's identity and are closely tied to the GNH philosophy. These vibrant and colorful events showcase the rich cultural heritage of Bhutan, with traditional music, dance, and costumes taking center stage. Travelers can immerse themselves in these festivities, experiencing the joy and togetherness that comes with celebrating Bhutanese culture.

For those seeking adventure, Bhutan offers a range of trekking and adventure tourism opportunities. The country's breathtaking landscapes, including the majestic Himalayas and pristine national parks, provide the perfect backdrop for outdoor enthusiasts. By promoting sustainable tourism practices, Bhutan ensures that its natural beauty and biodiversity are preserved for future generations.

Bhutan's commitment to biodiversity and wildlife conservation is another aspect that sets it apart. The country is home to rare and endangered species, such as the Bengal tiger and the black-necked crane. Travelers interested in wildlife conservation can visit protected areas and engage in activities that contribute to the preservation of Bhutan's unique ecosystems.

In the realm of health and well-being, Bhutanese traditional medicine and alternative healing practices have gained recognition both locally and internationally. Drawing upon ancient wisdom and natural remedies, Bhutanese traditional medicine offers a holistic approach to health, focusing on the balance of mind, body, and spirit. Travelers can explore traditional medicine centers and learn about the healing properties of Bhutanese herbs and therapies.

Bhutanese architecture and traditional building techniques showcase the country's commitment to sustainable development. The use of locally sourced materials and traditional construction methods not only preserves Bhutanese cultural heritage but also reduces the carbon footprint. Travelers can marvel at the intricate designs and craftsmanship of Bhutanese architecture, while also learning about sustainable building practices.

Lastly, Bhutanese textile and weaving traditions reflect the country's deep connection to its heritage. Travelers can visit weaving centers and witness the intricate process of creating traditional Bhutanese textiles, known as "thangkas." These vibrant and intricately woven fabrics are not only beautiful but also contribute to the economic empowerment of local communities.

In conclusion, the impact of GNH on Bhutanese society and economy is multifaceted and far-reaching. From fostering spiritual growth and preserving cultural traditions to promoting sustainable development and conservation, Bhutan's unique approach to happiness and well-being has created a harmonious and thriving society. Travelers have the opportunity to witness and engage with these aspects of Bhutanese life, immersing themselves in the country's rich heritage and contributing to its sustainable future.

Chapter 12: Conclusion: Embracing Sustainable Happiness in Bhutan

Reflecting on the lessons learned from Bhutan's sustainable practices

Bhutan, a small Himalayan kingdom nestled in the heart of the Eastern Himalayas, has become a beacon of hope for those seeking sustainable practices and a holistic approach to development. With its unique philosophy of Gross National Happiness (GNH), Bhutan has embraced a path towards sustainable happiness, prioritizing the well-being of its people and the environment. As travelers, we have the opportunity to learn valuable lessons from Bhutan's sustainable practices that can be applied in our own lives and communities.

One of the most significant lessons we can learn from Bhutan is the importance of preserving and nurturing Bhutanese spirituality and meditation practices. Bhutanese culture is deeply rooted in Buddhism, and meditation is an integral part of everyday life. By embracing mindfulness and incorporating meditation into our own lives, we can cultivate inner peace and well-being, leading to a more sustainable and fulfilling existence.

Bhutan's traditional arts and crafts are another area where valuable lessons can be learned. The Bhutanese people take immense pride in their craftsmanship, creating intricate and beautiful works of art. By supporting and appreciating the craftsmanship of Bhutanese artisans, we can encourage the preservation of these traditional skills and contribute to the sustainability of Bhutanese arts and crafts.

Bhutanese cuisine and culinary traditions offer yet another avenue for exploration and learning. Bhutanese cuisine is known for its unique flavors and use of locally sourced ingredients. By incorporating sustainable and locally sourced ingredients into our own diets, we can reduce our ecological footprint and support local farmers and producers.

The vibrant festivals and cultural celebrations of Bhutan provide valuable insights into the importance of community and cultural preservation. By participating in these festivities, we can learn about the significance of maintaining cultural heritage and fostering a sense of belonging within our own communities.

For those seeking adventure, Bhutan's trekking and adventure tourism offer thrilling experiences while promoting environmental conservation. By treading lightly and respecting the natural environment, we can appreciate the beauty of Bhutan's biodiversity and contribute to its preservation.

Bhutan's traditional medicine and alternative healing practices offer a different perspective on healthcare and well-being. By exploring these practices, we can gain insights into the importance of holistic approaches to health, incorporating both physical and mental well-being.

Bhutanese architecture and traditional building techniques showcase the harmony between human-made structures and the natural environment. By adopting sustainable building practices and considering ecological factors in our own constructions, we can create spaces that are in harmony with the surrounding environment.

Bhutanese textile and weaving traditions demonstrate the importance of preserving traditional skills and supporting local industries. By choosing sustainable and ethically sourced textiles, we can contribute to the preservation of these traditions while reducing our environmental impact.

Finally, Bhutan's commitment to sustainable development and the GNH philosophy provides a valuable lesson in creating a balanced and sustainable society. By considering the well-being of both people and the environment in our own decision-making processes, we can contribute to a more sustainable and happier world.

In conclusion, Bhutan's sustainable practices offer valuable lessons for travelers and enthusiasts of Bhutanese spirituality, arts and crafts, cuisine, festivals, trekking, biodiversity conservation, traditional medicine, architecture, textiles, and sustainable development. By reflecting on these lessons, we can incorporate sustainable practices into our own lives and contribute to a more sustainable and happy future.

Considering ways to incorporate sustainable happiness in our own lives

In the pursuit of happiness, our modern society often prioritizes material wealth, social status, and external achievements. However, true and lasting happiness goes beyond these superficial measures. Bhutan, a small Himalayan kingdom, has recognized this and has developed the concept of Gross National Happiness (GNH) as an alternative measure of progress. Bhutan's approach to sustainable happiness offers valuable insights that we can incorporate into our own lives.

One way to cultivate sustainable happiness is through Bhutanese spirituality and meditation practices. Bhutan is home to ancient Buddhist traditions that emphasize mindfulness, compassion, and inner peace. By dedicating time to meditation and spiritual practices, we can develop a deeper understanding of ourselves and our connection to the world around us, leading to greater contentment and sustainable happiness.

Bhutanese traditional arts and crafts also offer a pathway to sustainable happiness. These artistic expressions, such as painting, carving, and sculpture, are deeply rooted in Bhutanese culture and traditions. By exploring and embracing our own creative talents, we can tap into a source of joy and fulfillment that is independent of material possessions.

Engaging in artistic endeavors not only enhances our well-being but also promotes cultural preservation and sustainability.

Another avenue to sustainable happiness lies in Bhutanese cuisine and culinary traditions. Bhutanese food is known for its simplicity, use of local ingredients, and focus on balanced nutrition. By adopting a similar approach in our own lives, we can promote good health, support local agriculture, and reduce our carbon footprint. Exploring Bhutanese cuisine can also be a delightful journey of discovering new flavors and cultural appreciation.

Additionally, Bhutanese festivals and cultural celebrations provide opportunities for sustainable happiness. These vibrant events showcase the rich cultural heritage of the Bhutanese people and bring communities together in joyous celebrations. By actively participating in festivals and cultural events, we can connect with others, deepen our sense of belonging, and experience the uplifting power of collective happiness.

For those seeking adventure, Bhutanese trekking and adventure tourism offer a unique way to connect with nature and find sustainable happiness. Bhutan's breathtaking landscapes, including the majestic Himalayas, provide a backdrop for exhilarating outdoor activities such as hiking, trekking, and wildlife spotting. Engaging in eco-friendly tourism practices ensures that these natural wonders are preserved for future generations to enjoy, allowing us to find happiness in the harmony between humans and the environment.

Incorporating Bhutanese principles of sustainable development and Gross National Happiness philosophy in our own lives can lead to a more meaningful and fulfilling existence. By embracing mindfulness, creativity, cultural appreciation, connection with nature, and responsible tourism, we can cultivate sustainable happiness that transcends the fleeting pleasures of materialistic pursuits. Bhutan's wisdom offers a valuable guide on how to live more harmoniously with ourselves, others, and the world around us.

Final thoughts on Bhutan's inspiring journey towards sustainable happiness.

Final thoughts on Bhutan's inspiring journey towards sustainable happiness

Throughout this book, we have explored the fascinating journey of Bhutan towards sustainable happiness, a concept that goes beyond material wealth and focuses on the overall well-being of its people and the environment. Bhutan's unique approach to development, encapsulated in the philosophy of Gross National Happiness (GNH), has not only gained worldwide recognition but also serves as an inspiration for other nations seeking alternative models of progress.

One of the most striking aspects of Bhutanese spirituality and meditation practices is their seamless integration into everyday life. The peaceful monasteries nestled amidst the breathtaking landscapes of Bhutan offer a sanctuary for travelers seeking solace and a deeper connection with their inner selves. The practice of meditation, rooted in the country's rich spiritual heritage, serves as a means to cultivate mindfulness and find inner peace.

Bhutanese traditional arts and crafts also play a significant role in preserving the country's cultural identity. From intricate woodcarvings to vibrant paintings and traditional mask dances, these artistic expressions serve as a window to Bhutan's rich heritage. Travelers can immerse themselves in the world of Bhutanese craftsmanship, witnessing the skill and dedication of local artisans who have passed down their knowledge through generations.

No exploration of Bhutan would be complete without indulging in the country's unique culinary traditions. Bhutanese cuisine, with its flavorsome dishes like Ema Datshi (cheese and chili stew) and momos (dumplings), offers a delightful blend of spices and ingredients sourced from the fertile valleys. Travelers can savor the distinct flavors, experiencing the harmony between food and culture.

Bhutanese festivals and cultural celebrations provide a vibrant glimpse into the country's rich traditions and customs. From the colorful Paro Tshechu to the exhilarating Punakha Drubchen, these festivals are a testament to the Bhutanese people's deep-rooted sense of community and spirituality. Travelers can witness the joyous celebrations, immersing themselves in the contagious energy and traditional performances.

For those seeking adventure, Bhutan offers breathtaking trekking trails amidst its pristine landscapes. The opportunity to traverse the legendary Snowman Trek or explore the lush valleys of Bumthang provides an unforgettable experience. These treks not only showcase Bhutan's natural beauty but also promote sustainable tourism, ensuring the preservation of its fragile ecosystems.

Bhutan's commitment to biodiversity and wildlife conservation is commendable. With over 70% of its land designated as protected areas, the country serves as a sanctuary for rare and endangered species. Travelers can witness the majesty of Bhutan's wildlife, from the elusive snow leopard to the vibrant Himalayan monal, contributing to the conservation efforts through responsible tourism.

Bhutanese traditional medicine and alternative healing practices offer a holistic approach to healthcare. The country's ancient healing traditions, rooted in herbal remedies and mindfulness, provide an alternative perspective on well-being. Travelers can explore these practices, seeking rejuvenation and a deeper understanding of the mind-body connection.

The unique Bhutanese architecture, with its intricately designed dzongs and monasteries, reflects the country's deep reverence for tradition and harmony with nature. The use of traditional building techniques and materials ensures the preservation of Bhutan's architectural heritage. Travelers can marvel at the architectural wonders, witnessing the meticulous craftsmanship and attention to detail.

Bhutanese textile and weaving traditions, renowned for their intricate designs and vibrant colors, showcase the country's rich cultural heritage. Travelers can witness the painstaking process of hand-weaving, from sourcing the finest fibers to creating stunning patterns. By supporting these traditional crafts, travelers contribute to the preservation of Bhutan's textile heritage.

Finally, Bhutan's commitment to sustainable development and the philosophy of Gross National Happiness (GNH) serves as a beacon of hope for the world. By prioritizing the well-being of its people and the environment, Bhutan has become a model for sustainable progress. Travelers can learn from Bhutan's approach, finding inspiration to incorporate sustainability and happiness in their own lives.

In conclusion, Bhutan's inspiring journey towards sustainable happiness encompasses a wide range of experiences and values. From spirituality and meditation practices to traditional arts and crafts, cuisine, festivals, trekking, biodiversity conservation, traditional medicine, architecture, textiles, and sustainable development, Bhutan offers an enriching experience for travelers seeking a deeper connection with nature, culture, and the pursuit of happiness.